journey through breath

A Black Woman's
Meditation Guide
To Success

EZOLAAGBO ACHIKEOBI

Published by The X Press
6 Hoxton Square, London N1 6NU
Tel: 0171 729 1199
Fax: 0171 729 1771

Printed by Caledonian International Book Manufacturing Ltd,
Glasgow, UK.

Distributed in US by INBOOK, 1436 West Randolph Street, Chicago,
Illinois 60607, USA Orders 1-800 626 4330 Fax orders 1-800 334
3892

Distributed in UK by Turnaround Distribution, Unit 3, Olympia
Trading Estate,
Coburg Road, London N22 6TZ
Tel: 0181 829 3000
Fax: 0181 881 5088

ISBN 1-874509-76-X

a journey through breath

This book is dedicated to my ancestors Rashke Meneke, Kasamiya, Granil Rosalie and Granma
— great women of strength, love and character.

My beloved mother, Remah Joseph and beloved son, Kem Ra.

My spiritual guide and teacher Ra Un Nefer Amen.

I give thanks:

To Neter, the most High.

To the Neteru, the African deities who have opened my way.

To my ancestors — Rashke Meneke, Kasamiya, Granma Rosalie, and Granil who are always there for me through thick and thin. Whose divine light gave me the gift of this journey to give to you.

To all our ancestors who have showed strength, wisdom and courage in all they have done. Through their struggles we have been given the gift of life.

To Ra Un Nefer Amen, Divine King and head of the Ausar Auset Society whose returned ancient wisdom teachings have led me to a higher path and back to the source of my Power.

To Ausar Auset London, keep up the wonderful work.

To my mother. Mum I love you. Thank you for supporting me, giving me strength and encouragement at the moments when I most needed it.

To Tony and Jeffrey Joseph, my brothers. Thank you for always being there for me. I love you both.

To my son Kem Ra. My darling one day you will read this book and know that you were the source of my courage and inspiration. May the ancestors always guide you in all that you do.

To Michael Khesumaba Jess, who helped show me I have the strength to do it.

To New Initiatives, thank you for giving me my first chance.

To Mr Passion Incorporate. You know who you are. Thank you. Thank you. Thank you for the gift of touch. You have touched the pool of my spirit in so many ways.

To Cliffton McDonald. Wow, you pulled me out of the ditch and helped me up.

To Allen Williams for healing my life with herbs. Without them I would not have had the health to write and share this journey with you, my sisters.

To Jackee Trienu Holder. What a sister. Thank you for all your wonderful support. Keep up the good work you are doing with the sisters in London.

To Lorna Myries, who was there when I was broken. Thank you for being you; wonderful and magnificent.

To Chinweizu Foster, long may our friendship of love continue to prosper

To sister Augria, you always give me such sound advice.

To Carol Joseph for reflecting all of who I am and more.

T Khienda Hoji for giving me your endless support and legal help.

To Sherene Lee for allowing me to use your story. Thank you.

Finally I would like to say to all the sisters and brothers who have inspired me. If I have not mentioned your name, know that you have not been forgotten. I hold you always dear in my heart.

a journey through breath

INTRODUCTION

> *Guided by my heritage of love of beauty*
> *and respect for strength.*
>
> *In search of my mother's garden*
> *I found my own.*
> ALICE WALKER

I have travelled a long road to bring you this journey. I have traversed the road of pain, the path of doubt, the fear of doing. I have journeyed through the broken, resisted, fought, cussed, and tried to yell spirit right out of my life. There have been many times of writing when I stopped believing; stopped believing in the power, the light, the love of God. Stopped believing in the universal nurturing of the eternal spirit. In those times I refused to go within and went without. It left me in lack, a cripple without crutches. When I went without I went without Breath, I went without God, I went with resistance. So I journeyed without Breath, without universe's crutches. The pain got too much; the broken relationship, the low self-esteem, the overwhelming fear of single motherhood, all got too much and so I broke. There was no one to rescue me, no one who came to my aid but the eternal power of Breath.

1

Breath saved me. Like the devoted mother she nurtured me with the milk of life. She gave me new energy, a new mind, a new body a new purpose behind the pain. Breath released me from the thought that somehow life was out to get me and gently led me onto the road of spirit's healing. Without the sweet Mother's breath, I would not be here today sharing this power with you. I would not have had this unique life opportunity to travel through the darkness with you and come out into the light on the other side of wholeness. There is no wholeness without Breath, no unity, no grace. There is no peace without Breath. Without Breath, there is no ease, no journey, no stillness, no discovery of you — the You that really matters.

Who are you if not the divine awaiting its discovery? Who are you, if not the unique beautiful child of God? Close your eyes and ask the question and let God's simple gift of Breath show you the way. Breath is what will help you make the connection. It will release you from the imposed limitations of mind and life and take you into the universal spaciousness of spirit's dwelling. Breath will allow you, like a mountaineer, to risk the steep slopes and reach the beauty of the top. Through its grace, your life experiences will become beautiful lessons to reach into and learn from. Inspiration, creative opportunity, dynamic emergence into growth, will all be given to you by your friend Breath. The edge of pain and pool of joy will be made yours, too, as will the God within.

The God within. It is the journey we must make if

we are to claim our power. The God within is no white bearded white man sitting in the clear blue sky. The God within is not the malevolent punisher of evil doers. The God within is pure Love, Beauty, Harmony, Balance and more. The God within is a place where no limits reside, no doubts, fears or anxieties have a hold. The God within is omnipotent, omniscient, omnipresent. The God within is joy itself and bliss in abundance. The God within is the garden of your discovery overflowing with the scent of sweet spiritual inspiration. The God within is nothing more and nothing less than the divine intelligence that dwells within you. It is the place that will bring you back to healthful living. You can have it all, you can grasp it all, if you just STOP. Stop the rushing, stop the grasping, stop the resistance, stop the forward motion. Stop and sit down in the spirit of silence. Stop and rest in the golden hour of meditation. Stop. Inhale and exhale.

INHALE. EXHALE. Have the courage to move on. Have the courage to make the journey through the words and pages of this ancestral gift, and learn with Breath that you can tap the power within. Travel and discover *Lessons In Self.* Allow these ancient wisdom teachings to guide you to a higher place of knowing. Learn that you are more than what the eye beholds, more than what people have told you. Discover that you are a unique divine woman child of God with the power to match. Plant the seeds and enter self-mastery. Travel to the terrain of *Preparing Sacred Space.* Be like the lover going on a first romantic date and make ready for your place of meeting spirit. Travel into the sacred moment of *Golden Breath*. Learn, as the song goes, to 'breathe again'. Remember the way you breathed when you lay as a foetus in your mother's womb. Remember and reconnect back to the highest part of self — the indwelling divine.

Once you have mastered the lessons, once you have mastered the art of Breath, make ready to travel further and *Heal The Inner Child*.

Within each and every one of us is a child that has been bruised, damaged, rejected, and hurt. She is the part of our being that has lost its sense of '*I am*'ness. She is the us that needs Breath, needs nurturing, needs to go deep within and release the pain.

Release resistance. Look in the mirror of self, give the child within permission to grow, to see the light at the end of her tunnel and emerge into Love. Travel to *Awakening The Goddess*. Awaken the Divine Woman within, chant her words, inhale the healing power of her jasmined aroma and let the healing power of your spirit go deeper. Let the healing go so deep that your tears become a river, a sea, an ocean, a clean well from which your roots can drink. let the mother heal you. Let her nurture you. Let her make you whole. Let her show you the *Art of Living Joyfully*. God can be contacted with a smile, song and dance. Every road you travel needs the healing power of laughter and love. Travel with joy, lighten the load and make your healing journey fun.

Beware. Every road has its pitfalls. Travel and familiarize yourself with *Life*. Acquaint yourself with ego's bag of tricks, learn to apply the right antidote, and be a successful mediator.

Travelling is an act of love. It is a way of being, it is a way of doing, it is a way of healing, it is a time for *Affirmation.* Many of us wait for the day the journey will finish before we give ourselves permission to celebrate. We wait and we wait in frustration. Eventually we give up, concluding that life is conspiring against us. *Affirmation* is the rule of 'waiting' turned on its head and put the right side up. *Affirmation* is the power of gratitude that acknowledges your ability to create. It focuses your attention on what you have right now, so you can appreciate what you will have for the future. The more you affirm your journey, the more you will grow and awaken the magic of living.

Who is this journey through breath for? Who is it aimed at? Who can travel its depths? Who can enter the inner sanctums of its sacred healing? *A Journey Through Breath* is aimed at you — plum coloured, chocolate flavoured, caramel-painted black woman. As black women many of us feel meditation is not for us. We are made to feel alienated from its precious gift by those few elite and other cultures who want to claim it exclusively as their own. *A Journey Through Breath* is the power of the sacred gem returned back. It is the tool that came from the ancient black land of Kamit; the birth place of your Egyptian ancestors, and with love was given to the rest of the world. It is the jewel that belongs to no one religion, spiritual group or practice, it is the gift that belongs to everyone universally. If you are a Christian you can meditate, if you are a Muslim you can meditate, if you are a Buddhist you can meditate, if you are an African spiritualist practitioner you can meditate. If you are interested in the road to higher growth and spiritual enlightenment, meditation is the tool that will take you there.

Each stage of the Journey is specially designed to take you a little closer to Power. All you have to do is: Inhale. Exhale. Travel and have the courage to make the Journey.

A last word before you begin the journey. There is no such thing as an easy road. There is no road that does not hold its pain, there is no road that does not hold its tears, there is no road that does not require a deep persistent, inner commitment to healing and change. Keep the faith. Be Persistent. Be committed and you will get the pieces.

Ezolaagbo Achikeobi,
London 1999

THE JOURNEY

1. To travel is to stop your forward motion, breathe and go back to self.
2. Self is the unique creative You awaiting your discovery.
3. Strength, Power and Wisdom are your gifts from God.
4. When you take responsibility and commit to your journey, you commit to a life of change.
5. As you journey and heal, the universe will support you with strength, guidance and love. You will never be alone.
6. Travelling will open you up to a new self-power beyond measure. Claim it, embrace it, it is yours to have.
7. Refusing to make the journey will leave you stuck, bruised, limited, and unable to receive the magic.
8. Making the journey will fill your universe with love in abundance.
9. The journey is fun. It is represents a new creative way of doing, acting and being.
10. The journey is not about taking leaps, but small considered supported steps into magnificence.

CONTRACT

I _____ commit to making
my Journey Through Breath.

I _____ commit to the
whole duration of the process on the
understanding that there will be pain,
resistance and fear.

I_____ understand that
through taking responsibility and
travelling this journey I will be made
whole.

_____
(Signature)

_____
(Date)

1: LESSONS IN SELF

Our deepest fear is not that we are inadequate
Our deepest fear is that we are powerful beyond measure
It is our light, not our darkness that frightens us
We ask ourselves, who am I to be brilliant, gorgeous,
talented and fabulous?
Actually who are you not to be?
You are a child of God
Your playing small does not serve the world
There's nothing enlightened about shrinking so that other
people won't feel insecure around you
We are born to make manifest the glory of God that is
Within us
It's not just in some of us; it's in everyone
And as we let our own light shine we unconsciously give
other people the right to do the same
As we are liberated from our own fear, our presence
automatically liberates others.

MARIANNE WILLIAMSON
A Return To Love. Reflections on the principles of
A Course In Miracles

When was the last time you nurtured You, pampered You, loved You? When was the last time you put your arms around Self and gave Self a big warm loving hug?

As black women we find it so easy to do for others what we should be doing for ourselves. When it comes to giving to our children, our friends our husbands we are there on request with the band aid and kind words. When Self calls for the same kind of treatment, we frown and affirm 'my mother and grandmother got by just fine without any hugs and kisses'. Then we proceed to reel out our old tired worn-out excuses on why it hasn't been possible to find the time for Self first loving.

Often hidden behind the veil of our poor excuses is I-Don't-Love-Myselfilitis, which is the toxic syndrome that afflicts hundreds and thousands of black women across the world everyday. I-Don't-Love-Myselfilitis is a mask that hides our fear, anger, resentment, hurt and pain. Its origins can be traced to being repeatedly told as children, through deeds, words or actions we weren't good enough. For each of us the 'not good enough' reason took on different forms. For one person 'the not good enough' may have been 'you're not pretty enough', for another 'you're not smart enough'. However, it appeared you took the 'not good enough' as truth, sowed it into Spirit, held it as your belief, until you manifest its poison in every area of your life.

Whatever you were told about yourself in the past will shape your beliefs for today and the future.

Depending on the positive or negative value of its nature, your beliefs will make or break you. Toxic beliefs have us involved in toxic relationships, toxic friendships, toxic love. They have us envying, fighting and clawing our sister. Hating our brothers. Worst still we pass their toxicity onto our children and ruin their future.

If you looked deep into the mirror of your subconscious mind what would you find? Would you find the ugly duckling nobody will ever love, the fat kid in school who sticks out, the low achiever who could never meet (other people's ideas of) the expected grades? Simply put, if you examine your memory bank close enough you will you find negative childhood conditioning lurking behind its protective walls. Most of us choose not to look within, in fear of what we may find and, by so doing, forfeit a world of limitless potential. It will serve you well to commit to memory the warning: what you refuse to look at now will haunt you for the future.

Know thy self.

The World is Yours

When You Master

The Secret.

JUSTINA WOKOMA
Acts of Inspiration

Self knowledge is the universal light that illuminates another way of knowing. It is the constant truth Spirit craves over the illusory childhood misperceptions we hold of Self. It is the blue print that holds the secret keys to all you can be and more. Follow it wisely, make the connection, and enter abundance.

You can choose to change your beliefs now.

Do you recognise any Don't-Love-Myselfilitis symptoms operating in your life?
You wake up every morning and you feel:
Life is not worth going on with.
Loveless.
Empty.
Lonely.
Isolated.
De-motivated.
Depressed.
Fearful.
Confused.
Shy.
Ugly.
Tearful.
Not good enough.
A failure.
Pressured by other people's opinions of the way you should be, the way your life should be going.
Talentless.

Detached from your feelings.
Lost.
Indecisive.
Desperate.
Restless.
Angry.
Life is passing you by.

What you believe at this very moment, is just that — a set of beliefs and nothing more.

The mirror is a good place to start understanding what beliefs are holding you back. When you look into the mirror deeply, all you need to know about where you are with Self right now will be revealed. Unlike someone else's opinion which may be reliable or unreliable, the mirror does not lie, does not presume, does not have a hidden agenda. The mirror reflects what it sees accurately.

When Bernice came to one of my workshops she was in for a rude awakening. A fly sister with an impressive list of service to the community, Bernice hesitated when I asked her to look in the mirror. You may well wonder why. Looking in the mirror isn't easy when you have never looked before. Her courage and need for healing eventually eroded her fear and Bernice found the strength to look. Looking revealed to her the face of her dead father, rattling her into shock. Bernice's father had died some years ago but his painful legacy still lived on inside.

Like so many black parents, Bernice's father had

15

high expectations for his daughter, expectations which were his own failed dreams for himself. He wanted Bernice to be a doctor. Bernice had no interest in becoming a doctor, went against her father's wishes and became a successful community activist. He disowned her. Told her she was a 'no good failure'. She internalised his beliefs and took them on as her own. The result — she became blind to her own successes as she still sought her father's approval.

Bernice knew that to get out of the life rut she was in she would have to tune into Self knowledge.

In her book Creating Sacred Space With Feng Shui, Karen Kingston states mirrors are 'the aspirin of Feng Shui'. Mirrors are used for their power to bring more light into a home or more profit to a business. When positioned correctly in the home, a mirror can bring more light into gloomy areas. When hung opposite a shop till, a mirror can double business profit. In fact, mirrors are so powerful we are warned not to leave them lying haphazardly around the house.

What would looking in a mirror do for your life? What dark gloomy areas will it light? What goodness will it increase? Does the idea of looking throw you into panic? Does it fill you with fear? Does it cause the high walls of resistance to go up or do you feel calm acceptance?

Whatever you feel, know it is your inner child's way of communicating to you — she is in need of some love and affection. It is Spirit's drum call for some house clearing. It is a sign you are about to take a leap forward into power. Don't run, don't hide, don't panic and retreat back to your old self, don't do anything but embrace, trust and allow self to grow.

MIRROR EXERCISE

You will need:
A mirror.
Quiet space.
A spiritual journal to record your experiences.

INHALE AND EXHALE. Spend a few moments centring yourself with Breath. When you feel calm, open your eyes and pick up the mirror. Look deeply and sincerely into your reflection. Settle your gaze on your eyes. What do you see? Use this opportunity to tune into You. How do you feel about yourself?

Ask Self some questions: Are you happy? What is it you are in need of? What are the pre-dominant emotions and feelings you are feeling — love, hurt, anger, pain, joy? As you do the exercise you may feel resistance in the form of arising tension in the different parts of your body — your shoulders, back, stomach, head, legs. Do not try to fight it. Passively observe and acknowledge the place of its presence and quietly command the area of tension to relax. If you feel like crying — cry! Crying is good. Crying is about release. Crying is about recognition, cleansing and acceptance. Do it, for every tear shed you will release a thousand emotional toxins.

AFFIRMING SELF

Looking in the mirror can be a shocking experience. You will see things you did not expect to find. You will discover things you did not expect to be there. The things you have been busy suppressing and hiding from will suddenly make their presence known. Therefore it is important, after you have completed the exercise of looking in the mirror, that you affirm higher Self with positive and uplifting statements known as affirmations.

Close your eyes. Inhale and exhale. Feel all your surface tensions drain away with each breath you draw. When you feel sufficiently relaxed repeat any of the following positive statements or one of your own making to Self. Repeat it mentally three times. As you do so, visualise yourself surrounded by white light and enact their truth.

I allow love and acceptance into my life.

I am filled with universal love.

At my centre I am calm and at peace.

I love the whole of who I am.

I am powerful beyond measure.

I am a child of God.

I deserve.

Spirit nourishes and supports my growth.

I embrace change.

I am complete.

Today I enter into a higher place of love.

Know that, as you looked in the mirror, you were only viewing one dimension of your reality. There are two sides to every story. That truth also extends to you. Your reality is beyond the measures of what your eyes can perceive and what your mind has been conditioned to know. As James Baldwin said: 'I am what circumstances, history, have made me, certainly, but I am also, much more than that.' So are we all.

You may not be able to do this exercise the first time round. That's all right. There is no rush. There is no spiritual competition. Keep on attempting it. It will become easier with each new try. I promise.

I am an indivisible duality.

The real power behind whatever success I have now was something I found within myself — something that's in all of us, I think, a little piece of God just waiting to be discovered.

TINA TURNER

There is more to your existence than what you can feel, taste and see. There is a hidden part to your material existence awaiting your divine discovery. Like the sapphire stud I bought for myself as a treat, lost, spent hours searching for, only to find it waiting for me sparkling under the darkness of my bed.

The reality we are talking about was called Amen, Nu, Nut by our ancient Egyptian forefathers; Oludumare by our Yoruba parents. Whatever name you choose to call it, it is the other side of your story waiting to be told. It is the truth of your eternal nature. The aspect of Self you can feel, but do not know how to tap. It is the conscious part of you that has no beginning or end, no highs or lows. It is the you, free from the constrict of ego, fear, hate, anger, hurt, envy, insecurity. Your God. Consciousness is the truth of all of who you are. It is the power behind your earthly and spiritual throne. Tap into it and enter your queendom. Tap into it and watch your world expand, flourish and grow. Tap into it and watch your confidence soar. Tap into it and find your little piece of heaven on earth.

INHALE. EXHALE. Bring forth your God essence . Establish its rightful place in your life. Shout ego out and God in. Give Spirit — your eternal computer — back its rightful master. Stop re-enacting the programme of fear, pain and envy in your life. Make the universal conscious connection.

I am unlimited, powerful beyond measure.

> *Let us make man in our image.*
> **GENESIS 1:26**

If you are more than your world of limited definitions and the truth of all you are is universal consciousness, it is logical to conclude you, like millions of black women and men, possess a God nature. A God nature makes you a God woman on earth. Do you find this concept hard to accept? Do you find it sacrilegious? Why? Isn't it an honour to know that the creator endowed you, its child, with the divine power to create an enlightened way of life for yourself here on earth. As my spiritual teacher, Ra un Nefer Amen says, 'we are like God in the same way a drop of water is like the ocean. If you take a drop of water from the ocean and compare the two you will notice the two are the same in quality not quantity. We are the same as God in quality not quantity'.

We have been blessed with God's gifts: omnipotence, omniscience, omnipresence. Let's not fear them. Instead, let's aim to understand them, use them and make our lives and the world we live in a more harmonious place to be.

I trust and follow my inner Wisdom

We stay where wisdom abounds and the gospel is free.
FREEDOM JOURNAL NOV 2, 1827

You are filled with a magnificent knowing. You are filled with the sacred energy of divine wisdom. You are filled with the timeless understanding of God. You are blessed with the divine presence of an inner guide. You have heard its whisper in the stillness of Breath, the rustle of the trees. You have kept her counsel in moments of need. Sometimes you have listened and walked with peace, calm, and happiness. At those times you have made the right choices sprung from the clarity of right perception. There are also the times when you have chosen not to listen to wisdom's gentle voice, choosing the loud talk of ego over its quiet whisper. These are the times when you end up in a spiritual hole. You fall then wonder: how on earth did I get here? The answer is simple — you did not listen. You did not listen to the universe giving you wise counsel. You did not listen to the voice that knows how to turn apple into blood. You did not listen to the wisdom that knows how to keep your blood sugar level dropping below, or going above a sixtieth of an ounce for every pint of blood knowing that if it falls under, or goes above, you are in danger of going into a coma or suffering convulsions. You did not listen to the wise inner intuition that knows how to keep your breathing to eighteen or twenty breaths per minute or hold your body's temperature at a constant 98.4 degrees fahrenheit. You did not listen, and so you fell.

Listening can be hard. I know. Often I find it so hard to listen. I have grazed my knees when listening would have stopped me from falling. Society has taught us to value what we can see, what we can feel, what we can touch. It has taught us to grasp the talk of the rational mind. It has misdirected and mis-educated us to trust our misperceived notions from ill-gotten toxic belief systems. However, it has not taught us how to know and trust the subtle voice of inner knowing. Society has taught us badly at our spiritual expense.

INHALE. EXHALE. When you are sufficiently relaxed take your mind back to a time when you listened to that small whisper inside. What was the outcome? How did the incident you were counselled on turn out? Now take your mind back to another event and another and another. Remind yourself how your inner guide always works for your higher good.

In my workshops there are always those few die-hard participants who, despite everything they have been told, doubt the existence of their inner guide. For them the pendulum always came in handy. If you still find it hard to come to terms with the knowledge you possess, I suggest you purchase a pendulum from your holistic spiritualist shop or health magazine and do the following exercise:

INHALE. EXHALE until you feel completely relaxed.
Offer your pendulum for 'universal good'.
Relax your arms.
Hold the top of the pendulum string between the fingers of your right hand, or left if you are left-handed.

Make sure the pendulum is not swinging.

The pendulum is now ready to start working for you.

Ask your pendulum a question. Remember your pendulum can only answer 'yes' or 'know'.

First ask a rhetorical question such as 'Is my name (your name)'? This will give you your direction for yes.

Now ask the pendulum a question you would like to know the answer to.

The pendulum will swing anti-clockwise or clockwise in reply. Don't try to influence how the pendulum swings. Relax and trust.

I am powerful

> *I just say never mine, never mine,*
> *long as I can spell G-O-D*
> *I got somebody along.*
> **ALICE WALKER**

You have done it many times when you have felt the inability to go on. You have seen your mother do it, and your grandmother, too. You have listened to the praise songs, the stories about how your great, great grandmothers called upon it in the desperate darkness of their captivity. Strength is the blessing we all possess. Your inner strength is your omnipotent God power dwelling within. It is the rainbow serpent holding the egg of your creation tightly together with her tail. It is the potent inner source that goes beyond your world of limitations, beyond your cant's, maybes and I'm not good enoughs. Behind the walls of your doubts and fear.

Unlike temporal happiness that comes from external acquisition, inner power is constant. It is magnanimous, it is without fear, it is without grasping. Its ability to be present in your life does not depend on whether you own a brand new car, a brand new house, or a brand new boyfriend. It does not depend on things that can be given and taken away. It is the blessing that belongs to the pauper and the rich man, the child and the adult, the man and woman. All you need to do to manifest it is to believe you have it. Call on strength and live a life of magnificence.

INHALE. EXHALE. Allow your body to relax on each out-breath. When you are ready visualise a time when you were not ruled by the limitation of fear. Relive the scenario in its fullness. When you have finished, visualise another scenario and live that scenario in its fullness. Inhale and exhale. Open your eyes and know the strength you summoned at those moments of needs is the same strength that can be called upon in every moment in your life.

I am without limit.

> *'Pears like I prayed all de time, about my work,*
> *eberywhere;*
> *I was always talking to de Lord.*
> HARRIET TUBMAN

Next time you go walking, stand quietly on the land, gaze up at the sky, marvel at the stars, hug a tree or smell a flower, know you are witnessing the presence of God. Our ancestors embraced the belief that God lived in everything and everywhere. God was the wind, the sea, the teardrop, the rain, the sun, the stone. The power of God's presence resonated far and wide.

The ancient belief that the power of the creator could be seen in everything and felt everywhere expressed oneness. It expressed the belief that consciousness is without boundaries, limits or ends. It expressed the belief that, if God lives in a world of full expression, so do you, so do we all. As a child of the creator your world extends beyond your physical body. You are an unlimited creative expression, boundless in wealth, endless in potential.

INHALE. EXHALE. With each breath feel yourself expanding and filling your surrounding space. With each breath you grow larger and more magnificent, your essence expands further and further outward until you become one with the universe. Inhale. Exhale. know you can be anything you want as long as it is in line with divine timing and planning.

In the infinity of life where I dwell, I am whole, complete, and abundant. I am one with the universe and the indwelling intelligence that created me. I am powerful beyond measure. I have the divine tools to create a perfectly peaceful, happy and harmonious world for myself. I have the wisdom to confront life's many challenges. I have the power to go beyond fear and achieve what divine purpose has ordained for me. I have the presence of mind to live a clear, and focused and healthy life. I release the memories from the past that hold me back — fear, anger, envy and hurt, hate, pain, guilt, low self worth, and doubt. I release, I release, I release. In my release I accept my divine blessings from God, my father, God my mother. I come to appreciate the miracles and golden moments That shape my life. I affirm I am.
I use my free will to choose the higher way.

Behind each act of courage there is an unbreakable will.

ERIC V COPAGE

Every time I wake up for my early morning run, a battle ensues between my higher Self and my ego. On the battle ground are the 'shoulds' and 'shouldn'ts'. The shoulds are the whispers of the immense and immeasurable love which resides within all of us. The part of us that keeps us balanced and together. The part that cares about us and what we do to ourselves. The shouldn'ts belong to the 'devil's fork' which just wants to see us fall once again into the hell and brimstone of remorse, guilt, anger and failure. It is the part of you that tells you 'go ahead and indulge' in all the things that get you into trouble and keep you from moving forward in your life.

When you keep up with your spiritual practices, you strengthen the part of you that brings progress and happiness into the world. When you keep up with your nightly meditations, your daily yoga and prayers, you allow the immense inner light to shine and bring forth the power of your will in the fight against ego.

Every battle you win against ego is a victory for Self, a step forward in the right direction, a testimony to the great inner power that lies within and strength of your divine power to choose.

Before you give up, cave in, or simply sigh in despair. Know that it doesn't have to be that way. We all have the dynamic power of the will waiting on our property for us to use. Next time you need the courage to decide just think of a great eagle, the Kemetic symbol for Divine Will, residing inside of you ready to fly and fight at your command. When guided by the inner wisdom of Self, there are no battles we needn't lose, it all becomes a matter of choice

Lessons In Self

I let go with ease
I trust that as the old goes
A new brighter reality fills its place.
I welcomed the pain for I truly believed I was being re-
born again.
BABA IFA KARADA

The road you are about to travel will take you to Spirit's place of healing. It will transform and reshape you. It will move your journey forward. It will challenge your old perceptions of reality. It will challenge you to take a deep long look in the mirror. Sometimes the road will be hard, sometimes the road will be smooth. Always the road will challenge your deep commitment to change.

Changing can be hard. It can be frightening. It can make you want to run away and give up the gauntlet. It is a process of nature that facilitates a movement from pain to power. It is the prospect of pain that has most of us giving up enlightenment before we have even seen the light. As spiritual infants we are motivated by the avoidance of those necessary painful experiences instrumental in shaping our growth. We want to avoid those things that make us feel uncomfortable. Like children we want the growth without the examination. We want our lives to change without having to change ourselves. We want it all without the deep commitment to do all that is necessary to keep Spirit moving at the right speed in the right direction.

Yes there is pain in the journey. Yes there is the need for commitment. Commitment requires the deep embrace of responsibility. With responsibility you become the master of your own destiny.

When you feel like giving up on the path, meditate on the words of jazz musician Miles Davis: 'Bebop was about change, about evolution. It wasn't about standing still and becoming safe. If anybody wants to keep creating they have to be about change'.

INHALE. EXHALE. Know that as you take on the responsibility to change your life, universe will support your every need. Know that Spirit is not alone in its endeavours to manifest a higher existence. Know you have within all it takes to create a better and more divine universe. Inhale. Exhale. Move from a position of pain to power.

My small steps create my magnificent future.

Bit by bit we eat the head of the rat.
YORUBA PROVERB

Do you believe in instant weight loss, instant happiness, instant love? Do you believe that things will come at the click of your finger in an instant flash? Do you believe that if what you desire does not come now it is not worth waiting for at all? Do you leap before you can walk and run before you can crawl? Does depression visit you when something just isn't happening your way fast enough?

If any of the above sounds like you, you are suffering from 'it-ain't-happeningitis' and giving up before the going gets good.

I have seen it happen so many times on the road. More times than I care to mention — the happy traveller who reads a few empowerment books and expects instant transformation. She gets all uptight when the new calmer Self promised is still overshadowed by fear, anger and jealousy. She starts whining and complaining to herself and those around — the progress is slow. In fact it just ain't happening. She tells everyone, 'It's all a con'. In her immaturity she starts warning all to stay away from that spiritual stuff and stick with the old more familiar, even if it is damaging, ways of ego. She is the sister who needs to know: The higher path is for the slow footer. It is for those who can patiently put one foot in front of the other in the knowledge each step is a move forward in the right direction. It is for the knowing gardener who weeds and plants with tenderness and waits for the right moon before expecting to see growth.

It is for the sister who acknowledges small steps make big inroads. It is definitely not for the fast footer or over eager explorer.

INHALE. EXHALE. Walk your path one small step at a time. Know that you can be amongst the centred and powerful sisters you admire when you release yourself from the unreal expectations of expedient change. Relax and travel in a new, more joyful way. Change your perception and breathe in each moment of the journey.

> *The limitations you have and the negative things you*
> *internalise are products of the world. The things that*
> *empower you — the possibilities — come from within.*
> **LES BROWN**

> *That instant, it appeared to me as if a garment which had*
> *entirely enveloped my whole person, even to my fingers'*
> *ends, split at the crown of my head, and I was stripped*
> *away from me, passing like a shadow from sight when the*
> *glory of God seemed to cover me in its stead.*
> **JARENA LEE, 1836**

> *Our passage into queendom comes when we truly*
> *recognise that we are loving Spirit beings.*
> **OPRAH WINFREY**

> *If God be for us, who can be against us?*
> **ROMANS 8:31**

Modern man is in search of something which he seems to have lost. Curiously enough he does not know what actually he has lost. However he has a feeling that he misses something in his life without which his existence is devoid of meaning and significance.

ROHIT MEHTA

I am a unique person with a unique life purpose.

I think the human race does command its own destiny and that destiny can eventually embrace the stars.

LORRAINE HANSBERRY

Each and every one of us possesses a unique life purpose. Each and every one of us has been put on this earth for an ordained reason. Each and every one of us has a special skill, a special gift to give to the world.

Your unique life purpose can be found in the things you love to do. It is the job you do right now, the hobby you do in your spare time, the vision you dream. It is the things you express, the higher purpose you have come to fulfil.

When you have found your life purpose you will know. You will feel full, vital, alive. You will feel as though you are doing something worthwhile for humanity. You will do the work you have been ordained to do with love and ease. You will attract wealth and abundance into your life and have your inner higher yearning nourished.

When you are not fulfilling your life purpose you will know that too. You will find it hard to wake up in the mornings. Your vitality will be low. You will find it hard to smile or feel joyous about much. Every aspect of your life will be affected. Your relationships, friendships and social interactions will suffer as you feel empty and dissatisfied with your lot.

You will hear a small whispering voice urging you 'It's time to change, time to make a move. Time to conquer fear and move on, time to use your skills'. It's a voice that will nag you, nudge you, pester you and refuse to go away. It is a voice that may drive you into deep depression, feelings of unworthiness, emptiness, and despair. It is a voice that intends no harm, its only intention is to lift you out of your life rut. It is a voice that belongs to the keeper of Destiny.

Many of us find our life path when we are fed up with feeling fed up. When we get tired of that Monday-Morning-Don't-Want-To-Go-To-Work feeling. When we are not feeling too hot or satisfied within we begin to search for the missing keys. The journey towards finding your life goal may be short or it may be long. However, the journey to finding our life purpose is more simple than most of us realise. What the Divine intended for your life is often staring you right in the eye. It is that thing you feel so in tune with, it's easily overlooked. You love doing it so much you can't imagine it would make you a living. Surely, making a living has to feel hard, has to feel difficult, has to feel like shallow chest breathing — restrictive and dangerous for your health. This is not necessarily true. Life is as hard as we make it. Remember your thoughts create your reality.

Let's move away from the belief that life has to be hard, a struggle with no room for sweetness. Let's move away from the belief that we have nothing unique to offer the world. Let's create new thought patterns, new beliefs that tell us we have much to offer the world. We are unique children of God with a higher life purpose.

Fulfilling your life goal may not necessary include changing your job, or changing your lifestyle. It does not have to be done in huge leaps but can be done slowly and in small steps.

It can be expressed in all that you do as its purpose is to operate for the higher good in the service of others. Looking after your child and nurturing their higher spirituality can be an expression of your life goal.

INHALE. EXHALE. Make a list of all the jobs you have done in the past and present. What did you like about each job, what did you dislike? Did you enjoy working for someone else, or did you enjoy working on your own initiative? What hobbies do you have? What are the things that really hold your attention? Do you like to draw and paint or are you more into science, or both? Do you enjoy helping people or do you enjoy the challenge of organising and planning?

Re-read your list and begin to discover your life purpose.

I AM
I AM
I AM
I AM
I AM
I AM
I AM
I AM
I AM
I AM
I AM
I AM
I AM
I AM
WHOLE

Lessons In Self

Lord have mercy
Lord have mercy
Oh my soul

Lord I need thee
Lord I need thee
Save me Lord

Lord please answer
One more time

Heal my body
Make me whole

Cleanse my spirit
Make me pure

Send your power
Send your power
Right now Lord

WYATT TEE WALKER
Spirits That Dwell in Deep Wood, Volume 1: Prayer and Praise Hymns of the Black Religious Experience

The souls of old folks have a way of seein' things.
JEAN TOOMER

I will not allow one prejudiced person or one million or one hundred million, to blight my life. I will not let prejudice, or any of its attendant humiliations and injustices, bear me down to spiritual defeat. My inner life is mine, and I shall defend and maintain its integrity against all the powers of hell.
JAMES WELDON JOHNSON

Can't a man alive mistreat me, 'cause I know who I am.
ALBERTA HUNTER

On such a night as this, angelic forms are near;
In beauty unrevealed to us, they hover in the air.'
CHARLOTTE L. FORTEN GRIMKE

Ain't gonna let nobody turn me 'round. Gonna keep on walking, Lord, keep on talking, marching up to freedom land.
FREEDOM SONG,

She thinks her brown body has no glory. If she could dance naked under palm trees, and see her image in the river she would know.
WARING CUNEY

2: In the Spirit of Silence

*Strangely enough, the closest I've come to what I would
define as freedom was being deep in the hole (solitary
confinement) in San Quentin's Adjustment Centre. I had
been doing a lot of fasting — no meat, no nothing just
liquids. So it was during a deep, long fast and deep
meditation I found freedom that blew my mind. Right in
the middle of the hole, the deepest hole — the hole in a
hole. You didn't have a toilet, you didn't have a sink. You
had a hole. You had a bed that was really a slab of concrete
— like a gravestone. It was very oppressive. And here I
am free. It was the greatest time in all my life. It was
sweet; it was beautiful.*

GERONIMO JI JAGA PRATT
Essence interview, Nov 1997

Conversation with Self can only begin in the
precious moment of silence. It can only be heard
when the mad rushing has stopped and the ceaseless
thoughts halted. It is only then we can insperience the
tranquillity of the divine within and rest in the magic
of its stillness.

Many sisters who have attended my workshops
have admitted silence is the truth they fear. To be
silent is to be alone with Self. The fear is easy to
understand when we consider the world we live in
which fears the power of silence. It fears the power of
what it does not know. It fears the art and science of

'quiet time'. Quiet time allows us to take time out. It gives us deep moments of tranquillity and a look into our bliss. But who wants quiet time? We live in a society that has taught us to crave external stimulus and movement. When we are not working, we are thinking, we are chatting on the phone, we are cooking, we are watching the box, we are partying, we are listening to music, we are making love, but very rarely are we simply still.

We are moving. We are running from our darkest fears. We are hiding from the toxic beliefs holding us back and holding us down. We are seeking a false sense of definition and security in external acquisitions. We are travelling away from Spirit's centre and wearing ourselves down. Then we wonder why we stress out, break down and burn out. Why our marriages fall apart, relationships break up, friendships degenerate. Why we are bitching, arguing and hating. Why the bills never seem to be paid and the tax man wants to reclaim all you have made. Why everything around us is in disharmony and at dis-ease

> *Don't matter how fast you move, how fast you run, Spirit will come to claim its rest. You will stress out, break down, burn out until you return back to Silence.*

It was a law Sherene came face to face with. A hard-working sister with good looks to die for, Sherene had to get back down to some basics and quick. Looking radiant and positively beautiful did not mask her uncomfortable reality — cancer was eating away at her breast.

She discovered the intrusive lump early one morning while doing her routine breast check. Like the thousands of other black women across the country who repeat this daily ritual, Sherene did not expect to find anything. She had not found anything yesterday or the day before, why should she find anything today? But find she did. After the initial shock of discovery Sherene was faced with two choices — accept defeat and become a victim, or seize the opportunity and move into power. Sherene decided the latter and lived to tell the tale.

When Sherene walked into my four week Nu Life meditation empowerment workshop she was ready to accept Spirit's call to move into silence. She was committed to looking deep within so she did not have to go without. She faced the anger of failed past relationships, of her unfair treatment at work, the fear and apprehension she held towards her illness. She looked within and acknowledged all the things that held her back and away from the healing power of divine consciousness. Sherene did some house clearing. In the deep silence of meditation she pulled on her inner God strength and visualised the cancerous tissue, growing to the size of a pea, which had made its home in the part of the body we all fear loss. She meditated with the group, she meditated at home. She affirmed each and every living moment with a positive word, a positive action, a positive thought.

At the end of our four weeks together she went calmly to face her first medical check up. The doctors announced what in the West is called 'a miracle', what our ancestors called 'Spirit at work'. The malignant mass had decreased by 2cms. It had gone from 8 to 6cms in, what the doctors informed Sherene to be, record time. After the classes and for the following three months of her treatment, Sherene continued her commune with Spirit. She continued to meditate, embrace, release, and visualise. The cancer continued its rapid retreat.

The test came on the day her lumpsectomy was to be performed. Sherene braced herself knowing the 'divine within' never abandons. Sherene kept her faith and asked Spirit for strength. After the operation the doctors confirmed what Spirit already knew — the lump had reduced itself to the size of a pea.

Every day I meditate and I commune with God.

I am going to drink from the Crystal Fountains

And Move on up a little higher.

MAHALIA JACKSON,
Move On Up A Little Higher

Learning to commune with 'the magic' is the simplest most powerful gift you can give to Self. Connecting to your magnificence will, like Sherene, take you to a new place, a new experience, a new beginning of healing. In the holy moment of the 'grand silence' of meditation you will find the eternal balm for your life problems. Through the open door to its sacred temple you will glimpse your greatness. A greatness, as Sherene found out, will save your life.

Don't be like the many out there — satisfied with only glimpses of Self power. Build the daily practice of meditation into your life and make Self mastery your eternal way. Do as our ancient parents did and make enlightenment your life path. Breathe and stand in the peace of eternal grandeur.

So many of us live our lives caught up in a chain of endless reactions. Your husband shouts at you — you react. Your friend says something you don't particularly like — you react. Your daughter comes home pregnant — you react. Your boss tells you you're fired — you react. You screw up your face, you look murderous, you make your heart race, your stomach churn, your skin boil, you react and make yourself ill. Nobody has told you there is The Third Way of doing things. The Third Way of practising that will make your life better.

CLOSE YOUR EYES. INHALE. EXHALE. When you are relaxed go back to a time in your life when you reacted negatively. It could have been a time you received some bad news, a time when something bad happened to you, or simply a time when you couldn't stand the other woman who was up there in your face. Relive the scenario to its fullest. Experience all the tension you had then. See the colours, taste the taste, smell the smells. Make it real. Now relive the same scenario but this time you act the opposite way. You act from the peace of your higher Self. Note how the scenario turns out. How your mind, body and spirit react.

How did the first scenario make you feel? How did the second scenario make you feel? I can safely predict when you breathed fully and acted from a higher place everything turned out as universe intended — harmonious.

When you build meditation into your daily life routine you medicate your soul. You still the extraneous thoughts that steal your mental clarity and return back to life. Instead of breathing 25920 breaths in a day and spending most of your waking existence in externalised sleep, you breathe less, slower and live longer in the spirit of mindful awareness.

Check your breathing right now. Where is it at? Is it in your chest or in your abdomen? Close your eyes. Inhale. Exhale. When you are relaxed go back to a time when you were worried, fretting, or stressed out. Relive the scenario to its fullest. Passively observe where your breathing is.

When I get participants to do this exercise at my workshops they always claim their breathing seemed faster, shallower and centred around the chest. This is how we breathe in our hurried day to day lives. We move fast, think fast, breathe fast, and cut off our life force. Meditation says, instead of moving faster, let's move slower. Instead of finding the answers outside, let's go within. Instead of breathing till we're choking, let's breathe a little slower, a little bit more rhythmically and definitely from the abdomen.

Breathing from the abdomen is something babies do naturally, and what you did when you were in your mother's womb. It is the natural way and the best way to breathe, it is the way that helps us commune with Spirit. It is the way we breathe when we are relaxed, absorbed in reading, listening to music. It is the way we need to breathe when we need, like Sherene, to heal and return consciousness to home base.

When you feel stressed, angry, envious, depressed, at your lowest ebb, take a deep breath in, allow the air to gently fill your abdomen and INHALE. Pull your abdomen in and EXHALE. INHALE. EXHALE. INHALE. EXHALE. INHALE. EXHALE. Ease ego out and put universe back in control. Become the master of your destiny. Rest in the spirit of tranquillity. Insperience the essence of your true power.

In the meditation silence of my breath I have right perception and right action.

If you lay aside the ego's voice,
however loudly it may seem to call,
if you will not accept its
petty gifts that give you nothing that you really want,
if you will listen with an open mind,

> *that has not told you what salvation is;*
> *then you will hear the mighty voice of truth,*
> *quiet in power, strong in stillness,*
> *and completely certain in its message.*
>
> A COURSE IN MIRACLES

We have all done it; tried to find life answers while caught up in the mental gymnastics of 'what ifs', 'buts', 'should haves' and 'maybes'. We have butted our heads up against brick walls while bemoaning the fact the Creator has abandoned us. We have done all of this and more but very rarely do we think to step back, sit down, breathe and meditate. Sitting down to breathe seems too simple a solution for those of us who always expect life to be so hard.

But sitting down to breathe is what we all need to do when we want to see the fuller picture. Seeing the full picture is what the spiritual masters and gurus of our time have called 'right perception'. Right perception is the inward outward look of consciousness. We free our inner vision to look outward at the real picture. In meditation we see with clarity the things which would have escaped the external vision of our day to day eyes.

My problem had always been anger. Anger ruled my life. Anger lost me jobs, lost me relationships, lost me friends. Anger consumed me on the birth of my son. I was mad and boiling everyday. What started of as small bouts of anger towards my son's father turned into raging storms of screaming tantrums. I was angry at him when he left the place dirty, I was angry at him when he did not bring home the bacon, I was angry at him when he refused to help change nappies. Another day of screaming anger and violent crying made me realise I was an angry mess. It was then I realised it was time to go back to what I had been preaching to others. It was time to sit down, breathe, and take a look within. The healing of my anger began with a 21 day journey back to life.

The first few days of my meditation journey revealed a simple fact I had failed to see and failed to acknowledge — I was angry at my son's father not because he failed to bring home the money, not because he sometimes left the place unclean and definitely not because he occasionally refused to change dirty nappies. My anger was the mask that hid my true emotions of feeling unsupported, uncared for and unloved.

The rest of the 21 day journey took me to the internal birthing place of my angry responses. I had forgotten there had been a time in my life when I felt alone, trapped and misunderstood. It was a time when I was fourteen, young, fresh faced, fresh spirited, fresh from the Caribbean, and the new girl at an all white convent school. Used to having plenty of friends and good times, I did what I always did in a new environment — I reached out a hand of friendship to those around me only to find my offer rejected. The white girls found me too different to be respected and too exotic to be their friend. Instead of extending their friendship they made their choice and laughed at my cute colloquiums, they laughed at my accent, they laughed at my colour. While they laughed, the school's white teachers marked me down. Making me work the legendary 'three times as hard'. I grew from a socially positive young woman into a tantrum thrower. I threw tantrums at home and sulked and argued when someone said something I did not like.

In the mindful silence of meditation, Spirit made me relive my pain. With closed eyes, the huge energy ball of un-charged, un-claimed anger sprung from the depths of memory, announced its name, shocked my body and claimed my temple. For days I lived out its rage and cried hot tears. For seconds, minutes, hours and days I cried, wailed, bawled and allowed my body to cleanse, release, and come back to centre. By the end of my 21 day journey I had gained the clear vision of Spirit's right perception. I knew what action was to be taken.

Stepping back into Self gives us the time and space to see with the eye of our inner God. It gives us the ability to discern what is going on in our lives and steels us with the courage we need to remove the things that harm our conscious dwelling. Since my 21 day mindful awareness trip I have come to know Self better. I have learnt how to recognise when it/I am happy or in need. When anger or some other spirit threatening emotion attempts to rear its ugly head, I immediately pose my questions to the inner me:

Dear Self,
what is it you are in need of? What is it you are
not receiving? Tell me. Let me take responsibility,
go within and fulfil our needs.

Rightful perception informs us: No one person,
event, emotion, has control over our lives. No one
person, event or emotion can make us do what we do
not want to do. We have the keys to control our own
destiny. All we have to do is go within, and sacred
space will show us our lives. We must watch,
perceive, discern, then do what is right. We must be
responsible. We must claim what needs to be claimed
and get rid of the things that take us further away
from life.

I embraced this. Found the key to my anger and
enacted the rightful solution. I stopped blaming
others and began to Self love me first.

> *Being out of touch with our higher selves,*
> *makes us blame others*
>
> *Gives us a sense of Self superiority at a time when Self*
> *esteem is low. Stops us from looking in the mirror and*
> *asking how we contributed to the situation.*
> *Allows us to blame others and behave as victims in our*
> *lives when we are frightened to act.*
>
> SUSAN JEFFERS
> *Feel The Fear and Do It Anyway*

49

*In many African societies it is told in myths that
God and man were in close contact and
the heavens (or sky) and the earth were united.
For various reasons God became more distant
from the people.
Through worship man is able
to restore that original link.*

JOHN S. MBITI
Introduction to African Religion

———

*Returning consciousness to the subjective realm, its
original level enables man to go through life with
unassailable and with independent calmness.*

RA UN NEFER AMEN I,
**Metu Neter: The Great Oracle of Tehuti and The
Egyptian System of Spiritual Cultivation**

———

*When the consciousness is totally free from obstruction, it
automatically becomes fully aware and the person
awakens to full enlightenment.*

DALAI LAMA

———

*Meditation is a truly creative interval for here one gets the
intimidation of the un-manifest in terms of which the
manifest can find new direction of movement.*

ROHIT MEHTA
The Science of Meditation

———

In the Spirit of Silence

We must fearfully pull out of ourselves and look at and identify with our lives the living creativity some of our great-great grandmothers were not allowed to know.

ALICE WALKER

Meditate and learn to be alone without being lonely. Learn to be quiet enough to hear the sound of the genuine within yourself so that you can hear it in other people. A few minutes every hour, a half hour every day, a day, a month, a week a year — in dedicated silence — is a goal to pursue.

MARIAN WRIGHT EDELMAN
The Measure of Our Success

Herein dwells the still small voice to which my spiritual self is attuned. I find, also, that I am equally sensitive to any outside obstruction that would mar this harmony or destroy this fortress. These inspirational vibrations are known to me as my inner voice. Therefore, as I come face to face with tremendous problems and issues, I am geared immediately to these spiritual vibrations and they never fail me. The response is satisfying, though the demand may call for great courage and sacrifice.

MARY MCLEOD BETHUNE

*Taking time to experience ourselves in solitude
is one way that we can regain a sense of
the divine that can feel the spirit moving in our lives.
Solitude is essential
to the spiritual for it is there that we can
both commune with divine spirits and
listen to our inner voice.
One way to transform the lonely feeling t
hat overwhelms some of us is to enter
that lonely plane and find there a stillness
that enables us to hear the soul speak.*

bell hooks
Sisters of the Yam

———

*I am at my most peaceful when I'm enjoying sunrise
meditations, my fragrant candle-lit baths and spiritual
readings and tapes. But little by little the rituals that
sustain me are pushed aside as more and more of my time
and attention are demanded by the world.*

SUSAN L TAYLOR
In The Spirit

———

*Yes. You see, I was in serious pain for seventeen years and
there were three things I could do to get out of pain. One
was astral projection, or going internal.
The second thing I could do to get out of pain was my art.
The third was making love.*

RIUA AKINSHEGUN

INTERVIEW WITH JOYCE (NU LIFE WORKSHOP MEMBER)

Self: What was your life like before discovering meditation?

Joyce: I had a lot of anger. I had the attitude 'don't mess with me'. You see, as a child I did not know how to assert myself. I was the youngest of a large family of five. As I was the littlest, people would always tell me 'you're so cute'. I tried to live up to that sweet image. I was so busy being nice all the time that if someone was angry with me or did something negative I would have a delayed reaction. As I grew up I began to mask who I was. I was always on the defensive, always ready to cuss someone. I was angry all the time.

The way I was brought up not only affected how I related to people in general, it also affected how I related to my partners. I've never had an abuser, but I have had partners in my life who lean heavily in an emotional way. At the age of twenty I went out with someone for three and a half years. In that relationship I would not focus on my dreams. My ambitions. I took on the role of the mother. I was not taught how to love myself. My partner's needs became more important than my own. I would be more concerned if he had no dinner on the table than myself. I really played the role of wifey.

I eventually decided to break up that relationship. It was at the point when I was fed up with being the strong black woman. I was beginning to realise that being the strong black woman was making me miss out on so much of my life.

Self: What did meditation do for your feelings of Self worth?

Joyce: Meditation gave me Self realisation. It was like being given a golden key and turning that key. It was like opening Pandora's box and having an explosion. It made me realise I was somebody.

When I started to meditate it put down my defensive shields and saw I did not have to respond to things with anger. I could still wish people well even if I felt they had hurt me. It made me realise that having a mask and being so defensive about life was a heavy burden to carry. It made me realise that anger and defensiveness was not a solution. It made me see that even when I had cussed someone and put someone in their place nothing would be solved I would still be angry. Through my sitting practice I have learnt to feel compassion rather than anger towards others. We all have problems in our lives.

Meditation taught me where my need to mother my partners came from. It came from deep within my own yearning. I came to understand the nurturing and mothering I was giving to others was the nurturing and mothering I had always wanted from my own mother. My mother is a loving person but due to the way she was brought up by her parents she did not know how to show it in a physically demonstrative way. So I grew up craving affection and hugs. I grew up wanting to hear my mother say the words 'I love you'. Once I started to meditate I felt empowered. I knew that I did not have to wait for my mother to show me she loved me. I could show her how much I loved her. A few days after I had done a meditation session I found myself hugging my mum and telling her 'Mum, I love you'. She did not know how to respond. But I think she liked how it felt.

Self: What is the one gift you would say meditation has given to you?

Joyce: Peace. When I sit down and meditate I feel so peaceful. I'd rather choose the peace over the turbulence. I'd rather choose that way of feeling comfortable than being angry and cussing someone out.

The wonderful thing about meditating is that you realise everything you need comes from within. You realise what is right for you and what isn't. People's opinions meant so much to me before. But meditation has given me a fuller life perspective. It has made me realise that no one person can give me advice in every aspect of my life because that is impossible. I have learnt to keep counsel with Spirit.

In my silent meditation hour I remove anger. I remove fear. I remove resentment. I move closer to God.

We can only achieve enlightenment through the practice of meditation, without it there is no way we can transform the mind.

DALAI LAMA

Every time I see my old friends they say I have grown. I reply 'Yes, I've grown because I sit down, breathe, and meditate'. They look at me strange and then move on their way.

Unbeknown to many, meditation is a serious tool for change. Its power of transformation lies not only in its immediate ability to make the meditation practitioner feel centred, peaceful and more balanced, but also in its ability to purify the negative ego centred emotions that block our path to God.

God is our celestial internal light shining within. When our God energy lights our way there is nothing we cannot do. There is nothing we cannot achieve. There is nothing in life we cannot accomplish. Unfortunately there are many black women who have come to doubt their ability to manifest the power of their indwelling creation here on earth. We doubt, doubt, doubt. We choose to believe the God-less voice of society that defines us as 'this and that'. We choose to repeatedly live out the mother's voice from the past that told us we were born shy, awkward, slow. We choose and believe this is the way it will always be.

Universe has news for you. Your life does not have to be the way the rational mind imagines. You have as your gift from God the power to go within your mind, spirit, subconscious and transform your life essence into eternal light. You are shy now, but what about tomorrow? You are filled with fear today, but how about tomorrow? In the past you have lacked the confidence to make friends but does this have to be the case for the future? At this moment you may feel disillusioned, lost, confused, dejected stuck in a particular negative pattern or particular negative groove. You may feel you will never be like the many confident sisters you see. If that is your truth right now, fine, don't beat up on yourself. Give up resistance, relax, read on and learn to insperience a new truth about yourself.

Everything you believe about yourself right at this very moment was given to you by a parent, teacher, guardian, abuser... at some point in your past. It was most probably a time when you were extremely young, extremely vulnerable, extremely unknowing about the existence of another truth. After constant reiteration you internalised society's misperceptions and planted them into what our ancestors called Spirit, what the West call the subconscious mind. Universe informs us: Everything we have ever learnt stays within the memory bank of Spirit. Every second, minute and day of our lives we will re-enact the truth held there until we access it through the golden gate of meditation. Meditation is your gateway to Spirit.

When crossed, it is the bridge that will take you back to your past, the source of all your conditioning and help you see a new higher purpose into the inner realm of your existence.

The supremacy of meditation to act as a superior shaping tool in our lives over our normal functioning states of consciousness is explained by meditation master and high priest Ra Un Nefer Amen I, in his book Metu Neter vol 1: The Great Oracle of Tehuti and the Egyptian System of Spiritual Cultivation.

He explains:

The 'normal' waking state is characterised by the tendency of the will to impose itself over the mental functions and its command over the voluntary physical functions. In this state the will is primarily engaged in determining what ideas should be associated according to the sense of logic and reference to the person's belief system and what actions are to be allowed in the person's life.

The 'normal' dreaming state is characterised by the dormancy of the will which gives the spirit full control over the body and thought associations. The spirit's activities are of course determined by its programs, the condition of the blood, environmental influences etc.

In both states, the 'normal' waking and dreaming, the focus of consciousness is located in the external, lower part of being. A very important characteristic that they both share is their distructibility or the shortness of the concentration span. The inability to keep the attention on one object or train of thought for very long, during 'normal' waking and dreaming is very well known.

In the Spirit of Silence

Mediumistic or hypnotic (dream) trance, a state of meditation, is very much like the 'normal' dream state with the fundamental difference that consciousness is fully undistracted. It becomes totally focused on an object or stream of thoughts. This hyper-concentrated state of the focus of consciousness is the key to impressing upon the spirit the programs that will determine its activities. For example a thought to heal ourselves, expressed in the 'normal' waking state or dream state will fail simply because it was not held long enough in the sphere of awareness. In the mediumistic trance it can be held long enough to be strongly impressed upon the spirit.

INHALE. EXHALE. Close your eyes. Think about a time you wanted something and got it. Think about what you did to manifest its reality. Did you not close your eyes and visually form a picture of what it was you wanted? Did you not repeatedly relive your desire over and over again in the state of trance, unite your Divine Will with Spirit and plant its seed, like the planter, deep into the soil of your subconscious mind. What you did was meditate. Imagine what you can do, what you can create, the world you can bring into manifestation when you master its science fully!

I meditate and I am whole.

It's as if I've arrived in a place where it's all spirit and no body — an overwhelming sense of calm.
I actually began to feel blessed.
GLORIA NAYLOR

Are you stressing out, lacking energy, irritable, cussing and arguing for no reason? Have you forgotten what it is you had to get from the cupboard for the third time running, or are you simply a nervous wreck? If any of the above sound like you or if you want to prevent yourself becoming an exhausted mess — Rest.

In his book Super Nature, author Lyall Watson informs us:

> *The edge of a razor blade has a crystal structure. Crystals are almost alive, in that they grow by reproducing themselves. When a blade becomes blunted some of the crystals on the edge, where they are only one layer thick are rubbed off. Theoretically there is no reason why they should not replace themselves in time... Given time, the edges of the razor blade get once again sharp.*

If a razor blade needs rest in order to return back to its original state of efficiency, then the case for the human mind and body, made up of millions of living cells and tissue, needing rest is even stronger.

When you do not nurture your mind, body and spirit which receive and processes millions of external sensations every second of your day, with a daily programme of rest, you are heading down the slippery slope of ill health. Universe states: you can have all the money and material possessions in the world but without your health these things are worth nothing. Treasuring and guarding our health must become one of our life priorities.

Meditation is one of the most efficient modes of rest known to man. It is said to be better than sleep. In sleep our brain often works overtime as we dream about our work, relationship and financial problems. When this is the case we wake up feeling drained, fatigued and in need of more sleep. Meditation, on the other hand, gives our minds, and thus our bodies, complete rest from the external mental state of chaos, worrying and anxiety. Through its employment of deep, slow rhythmic breathing, it switches off the voluntary nervous system responsible for all our externalised activities of thinking, and switches our state of being over to the involuntary nervous system in charge of our internal activities of sleep, digestion, blood circulation, respiration and healing. Just fifteen minutes of meditation will leave your mind, body and spirit feeling pampered and wonderfully rested.

Not only will regular sessions of meditation have you feeling more rested, it will also balance the extreme negative emotions that make you boil and turn you green. All e-motions are energy in motion. We all need to experience more of the e-motions that send our energy vibrations soaring up, and less of the ones that bring them down. When you are joyful, happy and smiling, how do you feel? Don't you feel more healthy, optimistic, alive, creative and expansive? Don't you feel there is nothing that you cannot do and no fear you cannot conquer? When you are depressed and sad how does your body feel then?

Does it feel more sluggish, less able to go on, more prone to colds and other immune-related illness? Isn't it true you lose interest in living, Self, and others? Don't you just want to crawl into a corner to 'curl up and die'? For every e-motion we have there is a knock-on effect on our mental, physical and spiritual health.

By returning your stream of consciousness back to its original eternal state of bliss, meditation will go a long way to help you insperience more of the 'up' energy and less of the 'down' in your normal waking life. Combined with positive visualisation, meditation becomes a powerful tool for healthy living as Sherene's story affirmed. Sherene's experience of anger and breast cancer also helps us to understand that for every negative e-motion experienced there is a negative come-back effect felt in different areas of the body. The e-motions you have will either heal you or make you sick. What e-motions are playing havoc with your health of mind, body and spirit? Look at the chart below.

PROBLEM AREA	EMOTIONAL CAUSE
Headaches	Feelings of imperfection.
Ear Ache	Blocking out something you do not want to hear. Something that makes you angry, sad, frustrated.

Poor eye sight	Fear of seeing the present, future or past.
Stiff neck	Stubbornness. Inflexibility.
Sore throat	Fear of speaking up for Self.
Arms	Fear of embracing the new and letting go of the old.
Hands	Fear loss/not having enough.
Backache	Feeling unsupported.
Weak lungs	Resisting life experiences.
The Breast	Over protective mothering.
Heartache	Denial of love and joy.
Stomachache	Unable to digest new ideas or experiences.
Genitals	Feel sex is dirty or wrong.
Bladder	Pissed off with partner/life.
Colon	Inability to let go of wotless people.
Legs	Fear of moving forward.
Feet	Fear of moving forward.

Skin rash	**Feeling threatened by those around you.**
Obesity	**Seeking protection from hurt/ criticism. Lack of Self love.**
Anorexia	**Lack of Self love.**

In the silent moment of my golden breath I am transformed and the world around me grows magnificent.

> *I thought I could change the world. It took me a hundred years to figure out I can't change the world. I can only change me. And honey, that ain't easy, either.*
>
> THE DELANY SISTERS

We complain about the people and life situations we find ourselves in. We find there are people who enter our lives who are un-loving, unsupportive and down right abusive and disrespectful of our physical, mental and emotional space. Or we find we are constantly ending up in dead end or low paid jobs. We moan, bitch and wish things were different. But we do not look to how we can change ourselves. Change yourself and watch the world around you change.

For many years I was attracting the wrong men who were unsupportive, uncaring, and insensitive to my needs. Of course I did not feel responsible for this state of affairs. I thought something was wrong with the men. So I did not bother to look within. I gave each man an appropriate label: 'dog', 'bastard', 'abuser', 'waster', 'no gooder'. It was not until the break up of my last relationship that I decided to take a deep long silent look within to see what I could find. I found a small lost lonely child who had never learnt how to love and appreciate herself. A child who had never learnt to give herself Self love. This child was attracting men into her life who did nothing more than reflect the way she was feeling about Self. Wide-eyed and frightened I gently embraced her and surrounded her by the light of my inner love. I spent many days, weeks and months in the stillness of meditation drinking from the nourishing well of Spirit. With my mirror cleaned, the next man who came into my life reflected its light — he gave me lots and lots of love.

As you meditate and begin to turn your negative Self affirmations into positive ones you will notice how your new internal state of being will begin to reflect its magnificence into the essence of your external world. You will have the job, car, house, boyfriend, husband, lover friend that will mirror your new found sense of higher love. Your higher love will magnetise to you all that you need in your life.

INHALE. EXHALE. Close your eyes. When you feel relaxed go back to a time in your life when you felt unhappy with a person or situation. What was it about the individual or circumstance that made you feel that way? Now review what beliefs you were holding about yourself at the time. Was it 'I am not good enough/loveable enough/bright enough'? Reflect and see how those beliefs helped to magnetise that person or situation into your life. Inhale. Exhale. Know that as you change your light vibration, your external world will change.

Every day in holy silence I insperience my truth.

> *You cannot know what you will not taste.*
> WEST AFRICAN PROVERB

My spiritual teacher always states: 'Someone can tell you how an orange smells, what colour it is, what the skin looks like but you still cannot know what an orange is until you experience it for yourself'. The magnificent power of your inner beauty that dwells within is very much the same. You can go listen to other people's stories about it, you can go to your spiritual bookshop, buy up the shelves and read about it but you cannot know it until you taste it yourself.

Many doubt the gift of internal power. This was my recent experience of teaching a group of ten very sceptical Social Science BA degree students. Invited to their college campus to conduct a lecture on The Art Of Creative Relaxation, I proceeded to tell them all that I have told you so far — we are all unique children of God. We all possess an indwelling divine intelligence that makes each and every one of us powerful beyond measure. Meditation is the tool that takes us there.

They listened intently to every word I spoke then one by one went on to inform me why they did not believe any of it: If such internal power existed why had they never felt it? If they were omniscient, omnipotent, and omnipresent why didn't they feel as such? It all sounded very nice, they concluded, but it definitely did not sound true, and as for meditation, well...

I smiled. I listened patiently. I listened silently. I took them through a meditation session and they changed their minds. Every student down to the most sceptical had an insperience of the indwelling divine intelligence. As one female student, who had her initial problems grasping the notion of the existence of a God Self, put it 'When I meditated I had no thoughts, no nothing, I just was'.

The power that dwells within you must be insperienced by you. It cannot be accessed through books, videos, lectures, other peoples stories — these things can only awaken your curiosity and lead you to the well that only you can drink from. The only way to insperience your truth is to find a tool that helps you to do so. The only tool known to man is meditation. Meditation is the science of full internal viewing. It is the practice of silent sitting that turns the key, opens the door and gives you conscious access to sacred Self.

INHALE. EXHALE. Know that in the holy silence of Breath even you can experience the power that dwells within.

Go within each day and find the inner strength so that the world will not blow your candle out.

Meditation is not some strange or foreign practice that requires you to change your beliefs, your culture or your religion.
Meditation is not a religion, but rather a practical, scientific, and systematic technique for knowing yourself on all levels.
SWAMI RAMA

Tranquillity comes when we learn not to be influenced by external objects. A state of inner stillness must be reached in order to find peace.

I love to walk on the Sabbath, for all is so peaceful, the noise and labour of everyday life has ceased; and in perfect silence we can commune with nature and with Nature's God.
CHARLOTTE I. FORTEN

My life is actually better than it appears because of my inner peace. I used to be my own worst enemy. But that has changed.
OPRAH WINFREY

3: PREPARING SACRED SPACE

If you're going to play the game properly, learn every rule.
BARBARA JORDAN

The silent spaces we create in our lives are our sacred private moments of communion with the inner divinity.

They are the times we withdraw from our busy daily schedules and learn to just BE. They are the occasions when we give up resistance, worrying, fear, and tap into the wise nurturing voice within.

They are the golden intervals that belong to Self and you. Claim them and make them yours.

Approach them with the love, reverence, respect they deserve and reap the eternal benefits.

There is no such thing as someone who cannot meditate. There is, however, such a thing as someone who does not approach their practice with the respect they, and it, deserve. Being both mentally and physically unprepared they sit there and expect 'it' to happen, but meditation doesn't work that way. Yes, becoming one with Self is our birthright. We are made in the likeness of God. Going back to our true potential is our sole purpose. But you do not put a fish in a bowl with no water, food, plants, stones, and expect it to swim, much less live. Why do we think Spirit is any different? Why do we think Spirit does not require the right conditions to manifest its full glory? Spirit demands we give it respect through our libations, prayers, studies and above all our preparation.

Yes, Spirit likes preparation. Before you sit down and make your peace with Self there are certain requirements you must fulfil to make it 'right'. Making your sacred space right is like cooking your rice and peas on a Sunday. To make that finger-licking pot, those red beans, gungo peas, black eye peas, whatever peas you choose to use, must be soaked from the night before. On the day, set on a slow fire to simmer and cook all the way through, carefully seasoned and combined with just the right amount of rice.

If you do not prepare for your meditation session properly you will experience delays, discomfort, disillusionment, fear, frustration and you will give up. If, on the other hand, you take time out to prepare your surroundings, mind and body, you will reap tremendous benefits. You will be a successful meditator rather than an unsuccessful casualty.

Preparation is the key to unlocking my potential.

PREPARING YOUR SPACE

> *This is my space/I am not moving.*
> NTOZAKE SHANGE

Our grandmother's had a deep knowing when they

said 'Cleanliness is next to Godliness'. Spirit is reluctant to dwell in a dirty, cluttered place. Spirit needs a clear calm space to rest, energise and manifest its magnificence. Most of us understand this on a conscious and subconscious level. When you are in need of silence where do you go? To the builders yard, to the fun fair? A disco? No. You go to church, to the park, to a river. You go to a place where there is no noise, no fuss, no bother, no confusion — just silence. You go to a place where the mind, body and spirit can rest in natural silence.

To create a space for silent contemplation does not require you to do anything out of the ordinary. Chose a room or space in a room and make it conducive/make it free from clutter.

In her book Creating Sacred Space With Feng Shui, Karen Kingston warns that dirt and clutter in our external environment makes for dirt and clutter in the internal. Get out your polish and cloth now and get rid of dirt and clutter. Throw away unwanted magazines and papers, clean your ornaments, shampoo your carpet, mop your floor. Do whatever is necessary to help you and your space to breathe with ease. Just remember how good you felt when you last did that spring clean.

If you want to go one step further in 'lightening' up the vibe why not do to your place what your grandmother would do when the atmosphere got too heavy — a spiritual clean. When my grandmother felt things were not going right, or she just needed more harmony in her life, she started to clean. Like an

African priestess she would take out this, take out that, mix this, mix that, and begin to work her magic. She would wash down every wall, every ceiling, every door in the house while singing her hymns and praising her God.

Spiritual cleaning is something I used to scoff at, until one day my life reached breaking point. A recent graduate from university, I found and moved into my own apartment. Once in, everything imaginable seemed to go wrong. I ended up in a job I hated, which bore no resemblance to the career I wanted and, as a result, destroyed my health.

One day, on hearing my dilemmas, a good family friend suggested I gave my apartment a spiritual clean. 'This', he informed, 'will wash away all past and present accumulated negative vibes which come from previous occupants and have built up in the fabrics of the apartment wall'. He explained that every building needed an internal wash from time to time in much the same way we need frequent baths. Sceptical of the whole concept I put his advise on hold for six months. I tried everything else possible to make my life take an upward swing, but nothing worked. Things just seemed to go from bad to worse. One day I decided enough was enough. Enough of the boyfriend, the job, the unfocused drifting. I got ready to wash the negative vibes out of my flat.

Karen Kingston says our homes are like 'psychic rubbish bins'. The negative energy from all our previous occupiers arguments and ill feelings settle in its corners, nooks and crannies creating psychic cobwebs in very much the same way dust gathers and accumulates. She warns, 'psychic dirt' leaves no room for expansion in our lives.

If you are serious about your spiritual journey you must do whatever is necessary to invite the whole of life's magnificence in.

There are many ways to spiritually cleanse your home. Your grandmother, church or spiritual leader may have methods you may want to try. Below is a method passed on to me by Beke, a wonderful South African Shaman. It is one I use regularly.

To spiritually cleanse your place you will need:
clean clothes
clean cloth for washing your walls
olive oil
camphor blocks

MENTAL PREPARATION
Take off any jewellery you may be wearing, including your watch.
Remove your shoes.
Close your eyes.
Inhale and exhale gently.
Put yourself in a positive state of mind. Think of all the wonderful things you would like to enter your life and all the things you are ready to let go of.

It is a good idea to vacuum your floor and tidy your place before you begin. In a bowl, mix the olive oil and one camphor block together. Add some water. Use the solution to clean your walls, ceiling and floors. Start cleaning the walls first. Begin from the bottom and work your way up. Next, clean the ceiling and lastly the floor. Sprinkle difficult areas to reach, such as ceilings and corners, with water. Every room must be cleaned. Re-mix a fresh bowl of the cleaning solution and mix it in with your bath water. As you bathe, focus once more on all the things you want to attract into your life and all the things you want to release. Finish your focus by meditating on peace, harmony and spiritual growth.

PERSONALISE YOUR SPACE

Put up pictures, affirmations, sculptures, flowers, and anything else you can think of to aid in your spiritual focus. Below is a guide to the types of objects you can use.

CANDLES:

COLOUR	PURPOSE
White	To attract pure light.
Saffron	To open your way to success.
Yellow/Green	Attracts joy, creativity, spiritual/mental fertility.
Blue	To attract the healing energies of The Great Mother Goddess within.

Preparing Sacred Space

INCENSE:

SCENT	PURPOSE
Frankincense	Purifying aura of Self, object or space.
Lotus/ Sweet Almond	Deepen spiritual insight.
Lavender, Lily of The Valley	Open the way to success.
Anise	Aid in meditating on universal oneness.
Sandalwood Rose cinnamon	To attract joy, creativity, spiritual/mental fertility.
Jasmine	To attract healing.

FLOWERS AND PLANTS

TYPE	PURPOSE
Basil	To attract pure light.
Lavender	To open the way to success.
Aloe Vera	Attracts money. Deepens understanding of divine law of oneness.
Roses	To uplift. Attract joy, creativity, spiritual, mental fertility.
Lily of the Valley	To attract healing energy of Mother Goddess.

SACRED OBJECTS

TYPE	PURPOSE
Crocodile/monkey	To open the way to success.
Scales	To re-remember divine law and need for balance.
Peacock feathers	Attract creativity, joy, spiritual and mental fertility
Cowrie shells	Attract healing energy of Mother Goddess.
Akwaba doll	Attract healing energy of Mother Goddess.

GEMS

TYPE	PURPOSE
Emerald	To open the way to success.
Yellow sapphire/ lapis lazuli	Meditating on oneness, divine law, balance, outlook on life.
Diamond/white rose/ coral	Inspire creativity, joy, spiritual and mental fertility.
Pearls, moon stone	Awaken healing energy of the Mother Goddess.
Amethyst	Mental and spiritual clarity.

SET UP A HEALING SHRINE

Most of us have been raised to think of shrines as evil, no good, playing with trouble. But the above notions are far from true. A shrine is the most precious sacred item you can set up in your meditation room. It is that which symbolises the connection between the sacred and ordinary and re-members them into their rightful whole.

When I return home from the chaotic outside world of work, fast food, fast cars, fast life, and sit down to meditate, my shrine centres me. It re-members me and re-awakens my mind to the mantra I AM. I am more than what the world defines me as. I am a child of God, divine and magnificent. It invites Spirit and the many benevolent ancestors that work in my life to come and make me right.

I recommend the Auset healing shrine, and encourage all workshop participants to set one up in their meditation space. It can be large or small. Modest or grand. Size does not matter. Intention is what counts.

Your healing shrine is devoted to the mother within who gave birth to of all God's divine children. The healer revered by our ancient Egyptian ancestors and the rest of the ancient world. Create it in your space and invoke the essence of all God intended you to be — a beautiful black woman.

To create your shrine, place the following objects on a table covered in blue cloth:

seven white/blue candles
white lily of the valley
cowrie shells, sea shells
a vessel of water
akwaba doll
a water melon/cucumber/lettuce (choose one)

> burn jasmine incense
> moon stone/pearl

Once created, do not let anyone touch your shrine.

PHYSICAL PREPARATION
> *The body is the firm foundation of the mind.*
> MENG MING-DAO

Release tension. Before embarking on your practice session aim to release all tension and stress locked in your gross muscles and nervous system and built up over the day. Take a little time out to relax and stretch and reap the benefits. If your body is tense and aching all over and you attempt to sit down and meditate it will be a half achieved effort.

Loosen up with the following suggestions:

Take a nice warm bath with your favourite aromatherapy oil.

Stretch. Stretch. Stretch. You don't have to do anything complicated. The aim is to stretch the different parts of your body — arms, back, legs, necks — that hold in tension.

HAVE AN EMPTY STOMACH.
'Can I eat before meditating'? is the question people often ask. My reply is 'Can you swim on a full

stomach'? Like swimming on a full stomach it is not possible to meditate when your digestive system is packed with food and hard at work. Leave a gap of two to three hours after eating your last meal before you sit in contemplation.

No Drink. No Drugs.
The advise is simple. Do not meditate if you have been drinking or taking drugs. In fact if you are a habitual drug user do not meditate until you have dealt with your habit. Meditation demands as clean a temple as possible. Abusive substances are just that, they abuse the mind, clog up your energy, agitate your system, distract and dull the mind and senses. Hardly a conducive state for spiritual growth and insight.

The only equipment you will need for your meditation session is clean loose comfortable clothing. A warm room, chair and cushion.

Mental Preparation

> *You cannot shave a man's head in his absence.*
> **Yoruba Proverb**

Find The Time
I remember once asking a friend 'Why do people find the time for all the bad things in life and none for the good'?

Many of us find time to smoke, booze, over indulge in food and sex and make our bodies sick. Then, by some quirk of nature, time disappears when we decide to do what is right for Self: exercise, eat right, sleep more. If, as women, we took half the time we use making ourselves sick, and invest it in making ourselves well, we would see leaps of improvement in our lives and health. Instead we make excuses and say 'not today, maybe tomorrow'.

Not finding time for Self is nothing more than ego resisting change. Ego knows growth will topple its throne and ease the divine in. Know this, and make a deep commitment to fight for Self. Vow to put daily set time aside from your busy schedule to do some 'me first' loving. Make the time you meditate today, the time you will meditate tomorrow and everyday from now on. Consistency will remedy the mother of all evils — procrastination. Procrastination is the mask of fear and ego's desire to hold on. Daily consistent practice will help you to push through the barriers. It will aid you in your spiritual journey to a new higher you.

RIGHT TIME

Meditation enthusiasts often ask 'Is there a best time to meditate'? The answer is a resounding 'yes'. First thing in the mornin/almost last thing at night.

In their book *Fit For Life*, Harvey and Marilyn Diamond explain the body has three natural cycles: appropriation (eating and digestion), assimilation (absorption and use), elimination (removal of body wastes and food debris). Each cycle takes place at a set time each day: noon to 8p.m. — appropriation, 8p.m. to 4a.m. — assimilation, 4 a.m. to noon — elimination. When we work against these cycles we work against our bodies natural state of health. Working alongside them keeps us healthy and in tune with the natural rhythm of balance.

Meditation works on the same principle. When we meditate first thing in the morning we tune into the body's natural cycle of elimination of waste and toxic matter. This is why it is often said that, to meditate in the morning is to start your day with a clear head and balanced vision. While morning sitting is very good, night time sitting is very deep. As my grandmother used to say, at night 'the spirits come out to play'. Meditating between the hours of 8p.m. and 10p.m., the hours of assimilation, is very good for gaining spiritual insight and impressing things onto your spirit.

LENGTH OF SITTING
On returning to the Caribbean after thirteen years of absence, my father declared me 'neurotic'. His comment was a response to my exasperating inability to stay in one place for any length of time.

For those of us who have grown up and spent most of our child and adult lives in the West, staying in one place for a given period of time seems near impossible. We have been taught that if we stay in one place for too long we will miss the gravy boat. We will miss out on that man we have been trying to catch for months, that dream house now up for sale, the longed-for job promotion. We will miss out on life.

This attitude of 'can't stopism' naturally carries over into the beginner's attempt to meditate. Initially even five minutes of sitting feels like a chore as the mind races ahead of itself. This is why it is recommended that the new meditator begins with five to fifteen minutes of daily practice gradually building up to thirty minutes, an hour, and maybe two after six months.

DISTRACTING THOUGHTS

Distracting thoughts are the biggest problem for first time meditators. They just seem to keep on coming, making the beginner conclude 'emptiness' does not exist.

To avoid falling into this meditation trap yourself, it is important to understand the following facts:

In the first few minutes of sitting your thoughts will be at their busiest and most distracting.

Your thoughts will play havoc with your mind if you hook onto them. Practice being a passive observer. Let your thoughts dance, float and leap on by. It is hard at first but with time, patience and consistent practice it will become easier.

Thoughts become less intrusive after a few minutes of deep slow rhythmic abdominal breathing. Go back to a time when you were in deep concentration, when your breath was slower, more rhythmic and thoughts fewer.

Be patient, sit still, breathe, and know your thoughts will become less of a problem.

FUNNY SENSATIONS

My mother loves to tell me the sweet funny story of my youngest brother's 'first love'. Every time he saw his first love he would run up to my mum and confide his fingers were tingling and toes curling.

Having a liking for someone always brings with it those funny sensations. Our cheeks grow hotter, our bodies move differently, pupils dilate, eyelashes flutter. We feel that warm feeling in the centre of our belly, in the sensitive skin between our thighs all the way down to the tips of our toes.

Meditation is no different. Communing with Spirit has its own love chemistry going on. You may rock. You may sway. You may feel your toes and fingers tingling, or your body growing hot or going cold. You may feel large or small or feel like you're travelling across time. You may even see visions, light, hear sounds, receive messages. Or you may not experience any of the above and just insperience a deep inner state of calm. Whatever you feel, there are two things for sure: no two people experience exactly the same sensations and everyone will experience either heaviness or lightness, the two primary indicators that tell you have now been entranced.

Whatever it is you feel, see or hear, the most

important thing to remember is that these sensations are not the end goal in themselves. Do not hook onto them, or wish for them to stay, keep on breathing and aim for your goal — a higher place.

Awakening in the twilight hour

The moment of adjustment as the meditator opens her eyes and awakens to the outside world, is known as the twilight hour. In this sacred moment you may feel as though you have come out of a beautiful sleep. Do not rush back into the world. Enjoy the feeling and use the time to record your meditation experience. Don't procrastinate and put this task off and assign it to another hour or another day. Even though you will remember everything you saw and felt with precision now, if unrecorded it will become a faded memory in the mad rushing of your day.

4: GOLDEN BREATH

The Yoruba people say we were given two things by the God of destiny: What we came into this world to do and Breath. Breath is the elixir of life. Our ancient Egyptian forefathers believed it was the sail that took the deceased spirit to the other side of eternal life. That, through Breath, the deceased and the living could tap into the life giving properties of universal consciousness. That, by crossing its bridge, the internal and external could be linked back and be made one.

To forget how to breathe properly is to lose touch with who we really are. To lose the power of Breath is to lose the way to the well of our vast potentiality. Today we have forgotten the precious gift of how to use our breath to energise and vitalise our inner and outer lives. We do not inhale and exhale as we did from birth. Before we learnt what anger, jealousy, anxiety, stress and Self hate were, we knew how to control ego. We know the POWER of Breath. To breathe full and deep is to breathe in life. Do it now! INHALE life, EXHALE negative feelings. INHALE peace. EXHALE pain. INHALE love. EXHALE hate. INHALE and EXHALE. Ah, doesn't it feel good to breathe again? Doesn't it feel good to be alive?

Make a vow now to stop cheating yourself of one of the most sacred gifts you have been given by universe. Make a promise to Self to stop abusing Breath. Make a promise, a commitment to re-learn the ancient science of growth, transform and creative living. Tell Self you are now ready to breathe through your life with ease and grace. Learn to breathe again and hum in perfect harmony with Mother Earth's vibratory rate. Mother Earth is nurturing, protective and abundant. Imagine how your life will be when you tune into her heartbeat.

Every workshop I do I start with Breath. I teach the women who attend how to breathe again. To inhale and exhale in order to stop cutting off their own life force. I teach them that the key to inner transformation lies in the ability to re-master the breathing at a point one inch below the navel. I teach them when they are at peace Breath returns back to this place of its original centre. When they are out on an emotional limb it runs to the chest, cheating the mind, body and spirit of the vital life essence. I teach them what yogic philosophy teaches the universe — our days are numbered by the number of breaths we breathe in our lifetime. The slower more rhythmic Breath, the longer we live, the wiser we are, the easier we handle life's challenges.

KEY TO LIVING WITH EASE AND GRACE LIES WITH BREATH

This section will familiarise you with four simple meditation exercises aimed at teaching you correct breathing — the foundation for meditation, combined with the power of visualisation and words of affirmation. Each exercise will be taught over the period of a week and require fifteen to thirty minutes of your time each day. The mastery of these exercises will take you on a blissful journey to your next healing level: *Healing The Child Within*. Good Luck.

Before reading on, familiarise yourself with Chapter 3 *Preparing Sacred Space*.

INHALE

WEEK ONE: **GOLDEN BREATH MEDITATION**

> *Breathe again.*
> TONI BRAXTON

This sitting exercise will acquaint you with the meditation Breath. Mastering this powerful breathing technique is the key to attaining the deep sense of calm and peace we all desire.

DAY 1: **POSTURE**
Correct posture is the secret to correct breathing. Correct posture allows Breath and vital energy to flow freely throughout the body. Whatever posture you adopt for meditation must be comfortable and easy to accomplish. That is why the friendship pose is recommended for beginners. This posture allows the novice to meditate with little difficulty to the body.

The friendship pose requires you to:
Sit on a straight back chair. Hold your back straight. An erect back is one that has a natural curve

in the base of the spine. To obtain this sit on the edge of your chair, slouch and pull yourself up from the waist. Feel the base of your spine, it should have an inward curve. At first this posture may be uncomfortable to maintain as most of us are unaccustomed to an erect posture. If you find this is the case put a small pillow at the base of your spine. After a few sessions you may find that you no longer need a back support.

Keep your feet flat on the floor. Your feet have ten channels of energy flow in each leg. It is important to keep them in touch with the ground.

Rest your hands lightly on your laps with your palms pointing downwards. This prevents circulating energy from leaking out of your palms.

Keep your upper body — neck, shoulders arm and chest — free of tension. Lower your head slightly. Close your eyes

Throughout your day, practice this sitting posture. Where you notice points of tension in your body focus your mind on the area and mentally instruct it to relax.

DAY 2: **ABDOMINAL BREATHING**
The key to meditation lies in Breath. Your breath must start at one inch just below your abdomen. This form of diaphragmatic breathing induces a deep state of relaxation and inner rests.

To attain it you must:
Sit in the friendship pose. Breathe in through the nose, gently draw your breath downwards allow it to fill

your abdomen. To test that you are breathing into the abdomen keep your finger on the spot just one inch below your navel. When you inhale you should feel your finger rising.

Pause slightly. Exhale by slowly and gently pulling your abdomen in. As you do this allow the air to travel upward and be expelled through your nose. Repeat this cycle of breathing for 5-15 minutes throughout your day.

As most of us are used to breathing from the chest, you might not be able to imagine Breath coming from the abdomen. The crocodile pose is a good way to find out exactly what abdominal breathing should feel like:

lie on your stomach
point your feet upward
rest your forehead lightly on your arms
inhale and exhale deeply for five to ten minutes.
You will feel your abdomen rise and fall.

As you do your breathing exercises you may notice that you begin to rock, sway, feel heavy or light, and your breath may, of its own accord, begin to get slower and even stop. These are all very common signs that you are in a meditative state. One or two of these sensations, especially that of feeling heavier or lighter are normally experienced after breathing diaphramatically for fifteen minutes. Some people who are very receptive may experience these sensations much sooner, others may experience them much later. Either a few minutes later or after a few sessions.

You will soon discover which category you fall into. If it takes you much longer to experience these sensations, do not despair. Good practice is about being consistent and persistent.

DAY 3
Repeat day 2

Pay attention to any difficulties you experience. Write them in your spiritual journal. The idea is not to berate yourself but to keep a record of your progress.

DAY 4
On each exhalation you will allow all held tension to ease away making you sink into a forever deepened state of inner relaxation.

As you repeat this cycle of breathing you begin to insperience a deep sense of calm as your held-in tension begins to slip away. Every fibre of your being begins to feel soothed. The thoughts that arise in your sphere of awareness just float on by — you do not grasp at them, you do not hook onto them.

Breathe in universal love and allow yourself to sink deeper and deeper into a meditative state of tranquility.

To awaken from your meditation repeat silently to Self: I am becoming more and more awake. As I become more awake my eyelids feel lighter and will now begin to open.

When your eyes open you feel refreshed, vitalised and balanced. Rest in this beautiful insperience for a moment. When you feel ready record your experience in your journal.

DAY 5
Repeat day 4.

At the end of this session give yourself a huge hug. Self love is the best balm to soothe an ailing soul.

DAY 6
Repeat Day 5

DAY 7
Review your spiritual journal. What were the high points, what were the low points of this week's practice? Did you find it hard to concentrate, sit for a length of time, feel fatigued, find your thoughts kept on intruding and distracting you? As you continue your meditation practices you will find that the high points become more and the low points less. The best advice you can heed is practice, practice, practice. The more consistent and persistent you are with your sessions the more you will get out of them.

Many women find fatigue a great stumbling block to their meditation sittings. If you are one of them remember to do a few simple stretching exercises. These will serve to re-energise your system and get your vital energy moving from those stuck places.

You can also use the fingers of both hands to vigorously tap the top of your head. Yes, I know, it sounds pretty primitive. I remember when my master demonstrated this exercise to his students we just stared on incredulously. I know more than one of us thought, 'Is this guy serious'? He was, and we found that the method actually worked to literally wake up sleeping brain cells.

Deep abdominal breathing brings more oxygen to each cell in the body; helping the body to remain younger, more vital, and immune to stress and degenerative illnesses.

Deep abdominal breathing is the natural way to breathe. When we are foetuses in our mothers' wombs we breathed not from the chest but from the umbilical cord situated at the navel.

Deep abdominal breathing promotes greater concentration, clarity, and learning abilities.

Shallow rapid breathing from the chest starves the body of oxygen and vital life essence inducing stress and illness.

Shallow rapid breathing has been found by scientists to be the breathing pattern of people who are fearful and shy.

GOLDEN BREATH
WEEK TWO: **MUSCLE BY MUSCLE RELAXATION**

'I feel too tense to even breathe' is a common complaint often voiced by many of my students. If you have days like this here is an exercise that is guaranteed to de-stress you and ease you into the silent moment. Once mastered this exercise can be performed before each sitting practice as the need arises. It is also a good idea to record this exercise in your own voice onto a blank tape.

1. To begin. Breath gently and quietly for a few moments. Do not force your breath to come from the abdomen. For now breathe as your body wants to.

2. As you quietly inspire and expire, you feel the warm sensation of relaxation soothing the crown of your head. Inhale. Now exhale.

3. Feel the relaxation gently move from your crown to your forehead. Feel it spreading its balm starting from the middle of your forehead to its outermost region. As it does so you will notice the tension in this region slowly disintegrating. All worrying thoughts are washed away. Your forehead is now completely relaxed and tension free. Inhale. Exhale.

4. This wonderful feeling of relaxation now moves from your forehead into your eyelids. Its soothing touch works its way from the inside to the outermost part of this area. You feel the tension slip away. As it does so your eyelids become heavier and heavier and are completely and entirely relaxed. Inhale. Exhale.

5. Your jaw bone is tense. Knowing this, the restorative touch of Relaxation begins its work. Moving from your eyelids down to your jawbones it massages them easing the tension out. Feel your jawbones becoming slacker and slacker. Until they are entirely relaxed. Inhale. Exhale.

6. *The Relaxation moves gracefully into the neglected area of your neck. It gently kisses you along the entire column. Feel the held-in tension surrender to its loving touch. This part of your body now becomes completely and entirely relaxed. Inhale. Exhale.*

7. *As women we hold so much tension in our shoulders. Allow the Relaxation to spread into your left shoulder. The tension in this area slipping away, allow the feeling of Relaxation to travel down your left arm and now into your left hand all the way down to your fingertips. Your left shoulder and arm grows heavier as every nerve, cell, and muscle of this part of your body becomes completely and entirely relaxed. Inhale. Exhale.*

8. *Now allow the Relaxation to enter first into your right shoulder. Let it travel down your right arm all the way down into your right fingertips. With every in-breath and out-breath your right shoulder and arm completely and entirely relaxed. Inhale. Exhale*

9. *This deepening feeling of calm and relaxation now enters your chest area. As it does so your chest feels more and more relaxed. It expands. Your breathing becomes easier. Your chest is now totally relaxed and at ease. Inhale and Exhale.*

10. *The Relaxation moves quietly down into your abdomen.*

A warm sensation begins to grow inside of you. Visualise this sensation as a small ball of light which grows even warmer and larger with each inhalation and exhalation. Allow its warmth to expand, soothe and completely relax your stomach. Inhale and Exhale

11. The Relaxation now spreads into your pelvis. As it does so your pelvis becomes completely and entirely relaxed. Inhale and Exhale

12. The Relaxation now moves into your right leg. Allow its calming touch to slowly and seductively move into the top of your thigh and flow all the way down to the tips of your toes. As it does so feel each muscle in your right thigh, calf and foot become completely and entirely relaxed. Your right leg is now heavy with relaxation. Allow the same to happen with your left leg.

13. Now feel the Relaxation start at the top of your spine. Its journey begins at the base of your neck and eases its way down. As it does so you feel the tension leaving your spine. Each vertebrae becomes more tension free. Your spine is now completely relaxed. Inhale. Exhale

14. Your entire body is now completely relaxed. You have sunk into a very deep state of relaxation and rest.

If there is any part of your body which has become tense again just gently re-focus your mind to that area and command it to relax.
JUST ENJOY

WEEK THREE: **GOLDEN LIGHT MEDIATION**

> **I am the light of the world. That is my only
> function. That is why I am here.**

Standing in the cold night air I fought to keep the light
of the candle going. Each time the coast air blew it
out, I re-lit it with another light. In 1997 I was part of
a group of fifty men and women who meandered
down the steep cliff steps of Devon to pay respect to
the rediscovered ancestral souls who had sunk with
The London slave ship over three hundred years ago.
We vowed to them and each other to always keep the
light burning.

There can be no ancestral ritual performed
without the burning of natural light. There can be no
ancestral ritual performed without the pledge to keep
that light alive. Light is the natural centre of our
being. It is our ability to love, forgive and give. It is all
that is creative, illuminating and magnificent within.
To hide your light, run away from it, or allow others
to steal it is to disconnect from the most precious gift
the universe has given to you — uniqueness. Your
uniqueness is the embodiment of all universal
consciousness packed within your earthly shell. It is
the source of everything you are — now, tomorrow
and yesterday.

No two lights shine in the same way in much the
same way no two artists draw in exactly the same
style. You are uniquely different from the person
standing next to you. Steppin' into the light is a step

forward into Self and a step backward out of disunion with Spirit.

With every workshop I do I find the Golden Light meditation one of the most powerful. It leaves each and every woman with that warm inner peace of Spirit.

It is a meditation that is most effective when practiced for a minimum of twenty to thirty minutes against the backdrop of tranquil music.

1. *Begin by taking three deep inhalations and exhalations.*

2. *Inhale and exhale quietly and gently through your nose and go through the muscle by muscle relaxation technique introduced to you in the previous week. Remember to work your way from the top of the head all the way down to your toes. The aim is to rid every muscle, nerve, and tissue in your body of tension.*

3. *You are now feeling much calmer and more relaxed. For the next five to ten minutes allow your deep abdominal breathing to take you to an even deeper state of inner relaxation. With each out-breath, feel any residue of tension float away and leave your body. Allow your body to come to its natural state of rest. Do not fight the feeling. By allowing yourself to be in the moment you will put a stop to all intrusive thoughts that threaten your time.*

4. *When your spirit feels ready, gently re-focus your attention back to the top of your head. Visualise a white*

light entering at this point. Feel its calming influence spread slowly into your forehead, your eyelids, your lips, until it has engulfed your entire face in a flood of light.

With ease the light enters every nerve, muscle and tissue in your body. It spreads into your neck, shoulders, arms, hands and fingers.

With each inhalation and exhalation you draw the light forever downward. It now enters your chest and abdomen. Your whole upper torso is now filled and surrounded by healing white light.

The light now begins to journey into your hip, down your thighs, into your feet and toes.

Every part of you is now engulfed in bright white light. As you inhale and exhale, let yourself go and allow yourself to sink deeper into its centring influence. When you feel ready, your eyes will slowly open. You will feel refreshed, invigorated, and whole. Sit and enjoy this experience for awhile.

REVIEW

Write down: obstacles, insights, highlights and anything else that happened during your meditation.

WEEK FOUR: **AFFIRMATION MEDITATION**

To be a great champion you must believe you are the best. If you're not, pretend you are.

MUHAMMAD ALI

The law of Karma says 'what you send out is what you get back'. The thoughts and words you send out to the universe are the shaping forces of the world you create for yourself. If you believe 'you do not deserve', this is the message the universal consciousness will receive and send back to you. Your plans, your ideas, your relationships will amount to the messages you send out. When you focus on the thought 'I do not deserve', you are telling the universe, do not send me abundance, do not send me happiness, do not send me health and longevity because 'I do not deserve'.

'I do not deserve' was my negative affirmation. I always seemed to have money problems. I was always broke, and when I did have some money it seemed to, as if by magic, slip through my fingers. One day, in a bid to discover what it was about me and money, I sat down in a quiet moment and asked Spirit for the answers. 'I do not deserve' flashed before me in bold neon letters. The revelation stunned me. Hadn't I always told the universal intelligence 'I am open to a life of abundance'? Hadn't I always expressed a wish for a comfortable life to help me carry out my spiritual work with more efficiency? When I cut through all the 'hadn't I's' I realised that all the time I had been asking the universe to send me abundance, deep in my subconscious I was sending out the message: I will always be poor, I will always be struggling, I do not deserve my life to be any other way, and that is exactly what was sent back to me.

DAY 1: **AFFIRMING SELF**

'I am too skinny', 'I am too fat', 'I am ugly', 'I am not good enough'. What statements do you say to negatively affirm yourself? Listen to your inner voice throughout this day. Listen to it without attachment just be a keen observer to your conversations with Self.

Keep a small notebook on you as you go about your daily duties. Write down a list of all the negative things you say to Self to block the abundant universal flow of love, inner peace, balance and harmony from replenishing your life. Think how these phrases have affected your life to date. Working with the following categories may help you:

> WORK/SCHOOL
> RELATIONSHIP
> SELF
> FAMILY

DAY 2: **REWRITE FOR CHANGE**

Now you have your list to work from, take twenty minutes out from your busy schedule to silently focus on the things you would most like to change in your life. You may find there is more than one area of your life you would like to transform. That's okay, but keep your list to a minimum of two things.

Once you have decided on your focus, look down the list you made on Day 1. Which of the statements do you repeat every time you think of the area of your life you would like to change? There may be other negative affirmations that come to mind. What are they? Write them down.

Your list may look something like this:

AREA	CHANGE
Relationships	I want to attract a kind and loving mate.
	NEGATIVE AFFIRMATION
	I'm not attractive enough. No one will ever love me.
Health	I want to be healthier.
	NEGATIVE AFFIRMATION
	I am too lazy to exercise
	I will always be overweight, it runs in the family.

All negative Self talk is a series of bad habits.

When you engage in Self-negating statements, whether out aloud or quietly within, you are engaging in a series of learnt bad habits. Like believing that drinking makes you more popular, being subservient in a relationship makes you more acceptable and loveable to your partner. You are not born with fearful talk, you learnt it along the way. You learnt to believe you are not attractive. You learnt to believe no one will love you because you are not worth loving. These beliefs are learnt from an external source. If you do not feel you are worth loving you may have had a parent who was never there for you, who never gave you the time of day or who just never gave you a hug. Not only did you learn this belief, you also internalised it and incorporated it into your belief system so it became an automatic part of your Self talk.

You are responsible for your life.

We said that all your negative Self talk is learnt from a source outside of yourself. This is not permission to go and blame someone else for the way you are. The other side of the rule to all learnt negative states — the point of change starts with you. You have been given all the divine faculties to change your life. You are responsible for all your behaviour.

Now you have identified the area of your life you want to change and the negative Self talk accompanying it, you can take steps to institute new positive affirmations in your life.

The rule to writing positive affirmations is:

Avoid negatives in writing your positive affirmation. Instead of saying 'I will not be lazy any more and will exercise' affirm 'Everyday I exercise with ease'.

Keep statements in the present. Instead of saying 'I will attract love into my life' affirm, 'I am open to the abundant flow of universal love'.

Keep statements in the first person.

It is important to have belief in your new Self statement.

Example:

AREA	NEGATIVE	POSITIVE
CHANGE	AFFIRMATION	AFFIRMATION
Love	I want to attract a kind and loving mate.	I'm too ugly to be loved.
	I am too old.	I am lovable.
		Today I am an open vessel that receives the abundant universal love.

DAY 3: WORKING WITH YOUR NEW STATEMENT

As every negative statement we repeat to Self is a bad habit rehearsed through constant repetition, your new positive affirmation must also be installed through repetition:

Repeat your positive affirmation out loud to yourself several hundred times for the day.

Place it in key areas — above your bathroom sink, on the wall of your work station, above your bed.

Remember, you must believe in what you are saying. At first what you are saying to Self may feel like a big lie. If you have always told your Self 'I am unlovable', telling yourself the opposite will feel a bit strange and like an untruth. Changing bad habits is always met with resistance. Ego always jumps in to stop the positive progress, but a deep commitment to change always forces fear, disbelief and those old mental habits to take a back seat.

DAY 4

Someone tells you how stupid you are, for that instant all thought and sometimes even your breath becomes suspended and the idea is taken into Spirit. The more you are told you are stupid, the more you internalise it, the more Spirit takes it on board as a fact whether it is true or not.

This is why meditation and hypnotherapy are such successful tools for character transformation. Both forms are based on inducing a deepened state of trance within the individual so it becomes possible to make connections between what spiritual practitioners call the spirit, and hypnotherapist call the subconscious mind. To access this part of our being is to get in touch with the master computer which holds the key to all our actions, words, and behaviour.

To repeat an affirmation in the meditative state is to re-programme that bad habit at the deepest level possible — the level of Spirit. This is what makes affirmation meditations so powerful.

In this meditation your new positive statement will be repeated both visually and verbally. Put aside thirty minutes of quiet time for yourself. It is also a nice idea to do this meditation with some gentle music playing in the background.

Engage in deep abdominal breathing for fifteen minutes. On the in-breath you will inhale deeply. As you breathe in you can feel yourself being filled up with the universal intelligence. On the out-breath you will expire slowly and feel all your tension draining away. On each exhalation you will become more and more relaxed.

When you are fifteen minutes into your breathing you will feel yourself becoming very light or very heavy, this is an indicator that you are in a state of trance.

Visualise a time when you were chastising yourself for being: 'too ugly, too skinny, not good enough'. Visualise it as if you are going through it now. As you do so, relive all your emotions, feelings, tensions that were involved in the scenario. Do this for a few minutes.

Now begin to re-enact this scenario in a more positive way. If you are trying to counteract negative feelings about your weight and your new positive affirmation is something like 'I love me just the way I am', visualise yourself giving yourself a hug, kissing your body, doing the things that you would do to indicate to a child that you love them.

When you are ready let this visualisation go and allow a white light to enter and engulf your body. It starts from the crown of your head and works its way all the way down to the tips of your toes. Feel it engulf and embrace you with love. As you sit peacefully in the white light repeat your affirmation silently to yourself.

Gently bring yourself out of this meditation by telling yourself 'My eyelids are now becoming lighter and lighter. They are so light they now begin to open'.

As you open your eyes you feel wonderfully relaxed, and at total peace.

DAY 5
Repeat the previous exercise.

DAY 6
Repeat day 5.

DAY 7
How was this exercise for you? What were your points of resistance? Where and how did they manifest themselves: in your stomach, in your shoulders, in your legs?

EXERCISE PURPOSE
1. Golden Breath Meditation — to acquaint you with deep abdominal breathing and to improve your inner state of well being.
2. Muscle by Muscle Relaxation — to release held tension in order to aid in the meditation practice.
3. Golden Light Meditation — to create a deep sense of well being and health.
4. Affirmation Meditation — to change negative Self and introduce visualisation.

5: HEALING THE INNER CHILD

Children are so quick. Quick to laugh, quick to brand,
quick to scorn, quick to lay claim to the open space.
JAMAICA KINCAID

Imagine you are a brilliant musician who has had a car accident. After the accident you do not remember anything about yourself, who you were, the people you knew, the places you lived, the ones you loved — all you know is what other people tell you about yourself. Unfortunately you are now living with a wicked stepmother who tells you how dumb, unlovable and untalented you are. You believe her because you do not remember anything else. A vague feeling within tells you there is something about you that is greater, but that is how it stays, a vague feeling. You go on to spend the rest of your adult life in misery and unfulfilled.

This sounds like a badly written far-fetched fairy tale, doesn't it? I know, but don't laugh. This story could be yours. Before you came into this world, before you entered the sacred space of your mother's womb, you were given a unique purpose and gifts to share with the world. But as your spirit grew and matured in the foetal waters of life, the memory of your mission became more and more lost in your subconscious memory bank. The divine intelligence never leaves anything wanting. It planned it that our parents and community were to be the loving eyes that mirrored and reminded us all of who we are.

Traditionally, as soon as a woman knew she was carrying a child a priest would be called to give her and the husband the child's destiny reading. An appropriate name would then be picked which would remind the child of her life purpose. On her birth she would hear her name. The toys and education given to her by the parents and community served one purpose — to nurture her universal gifts.

Today things are vastly different. Our parents and community do not have the guidance of the traditional village priest to inform them of our purpose. Their parents before them did not have this either. The result — generations of black women without a sense of what John Bradshaw, author of *Home Coming* referred to as 'reclaiming and championing your inner child', or 'I amness'. 'I amness' is the sense of wholeness we are born with when we are children. It is the seat of our spirituality. It is that which says 'I am divine, unlimited, unique, and special. I am here as a child of God'. When we have a sense of 'I amness' we are at ease with Life and its universal flow. Nothing seems an effort. Nothing seems impossible, frightening or daunting. The world suddenly becomes a wonderful place to explore discover and expand within

We desperately need to reclaim this sense of wholeness. It is the journey our inner child craves. It is the journey it needs to make. Like all bruised children she needs love, nurturing and you. Reach out and touch her now. Reassure her that together you will journey and make it back to the centre. Commit to her and Self, that you will be there for both of you every step of the way.

A warning. The journey into healing involves pain, yes, I won't lie, there is a lot of pain involved. Grief, yes, there is a lot of that too. There are many tears to be shed and memories to be relived. Without these medicines your spiritual wound cannot close, cannot get better, cannot find its place of healing. In Jamaica, the place of my mothers birth, there is a saying: 'Women, when a loved one dies hold your belly and wail'. There is no shame in it, no guilt, no resistance, it is the natural order of things, nature's response to healing. I have conducted many workshops where women have not wanted to look back, have not wanted to go through the old memories, have not wanted to go through the dark tunnel to grieve and shed tears. Sometimes they just aren't ready. Most of the time, though, resistance is in effect.

Change can seem frightening. Even though what we are holding onto is ruining our lives, it often feels less daunting than letting go.

To give up resistance is to take your first step into power. Through love you can do it. Love is the guide that lights your path back to universal wholeness. Make a statement to your inner child today, make it sound something like: 'Today I embrace you in the universal light of change and wholeness'. Change is okay. It's okay to change. A tree does not stay the same with every season, the earth does not stand still on its axis. All things were made by the universal life intelligence to change and grow. To change is to keep with the divine order of things.

We have talked long enough: we were now ready to move; if not now we never should be; and if we did not intend to move now we had as well fold our arms, sit down, and acknowledge ourselves fit only to be slaves.

FREDERICK DOUGLAS

When face to face with oneself, there is no cop-out.

EDWARD KENNEDY 'DUKE' ELLINGTON

MIRROR MIRROR ON THE WALL

You will remember in an earlier chapter Lessons in Self you were asked to take a look in the mirror. Some were able to do this exercise with ease, others not. The mirror is our true reflection. It reflects all that is happening in our lives right at this very moment. To look in the mirror is to face truth. To embrace truth is to embrace responsibility. You have the responsibility for changing your life, making it better, more dynamic — not your next door neighbour, not your lover, not your child — only you can make your life as you want it to be. What happened in the past happened. You cannot help that, but you can decide what happens to you from this moment on.

Take a few moments of this day to sit in silent contemplation and meet yourself in the mirror. For this exercise you will need a comfortable chair, a quiet room and a mirror.

Close your eyes and take a few deep breaths. Inhale and exhale. As you do so allow every muscle and nerve in your body to relax. Allow all the tension to drain away. Feel yourself sinking deeper and deeper into a state of inner relaxation. When you are ready, slowly open your eyes and look gently into the mirror. Look at every part of your face and allow your eyes to rest on their reflection. What do you see, what do you feel? Give yourself time, there is no hurry. Give permission to whatever emotions want to surface to go ahead and make their presence known. If you find there is resistance, that's okay, it's a natural ego response. It tells you change is near. Soften the hard edges resistance with love. Feel it melt away as you continue to meet Self in the mirror. Your inner child might feel panicked at what you find, reassure her that all is well, no harm will come to her.

If you are a victim of any form of sexual or physical abuse or an addict, please do not do this exercise or continue this chapter unless you have been or are under the guidance of a trained counsellor.

For women who do this exercise in my workshops all sorts of surprising, often shocking things are thrown up. One woman, a community activist, saw the face of her father. Her father had died three years prior to her doing the exercise. He had always wanted her to be a doctor. She ended up being involved in community affairs. She thought she had forgiven him for making her feel like a failure. She thought the pain had gone away, but there it was still staring her in the face. After the initial shock, came resistance and, finally, realisation that her father was the inner critic who still affected her life. No matter how well she excelled, she heard his voice whisper 'It's not good enough. You are a failure'. Through acceptance and forgiveness she was able to heal the pain.

Another woman, a full time single mother, saw the face of her mother. She was shocked at how much she looked like her. People had always commented on the fact but she had never stopped in front of the mirror long enough to notice. Her relationship with her mother had been fraught with difficulties and lovelessness. It was the pain she needed to heal to move on with her life.

One workshop participant repeated my four week workshop three times before she accepted the ugliness and evil she kept on seeing in the mirror was her scared inner child in need of healing from years of sexual abuse endured under the hands of her father. Her inner child was telling her I feel dirty, unclean, abused and unloved. I need you to love me. I need you to heal. Through her acceptance and a commitment to move on this particular workshop participant made massive leaps into Self mastery.

There is no time limit on this exercise. Do it in

your own time. Do not rush yourself. If you are having difficulties looking in the mirror, put it aside for a while and go back to it. Do persist. Resistance is a good sign. It is the body's way of letting us know there is something we need to let go of.

Repeat this exercise several times over the space of the next few weeks. After each session repeat a loving affirmation to your inner child. Let your intuition guide you on what to say, or use one of the many wonderful affirmation books available on the market.

Keep a record of your emotions, insights and feelings. What are the things that came up for you? You may have found you have a lot of unresolved anger, feel ugly, unloved, not good enough, whatever the feelings you felt, write them down. They are the ones you need to heal.

> *History is our guide.*
> *Without a knowledge of it, we are lost.*
> LOUIS FARRAKHAN

ORIGINAL PAIN

Part of healing the pain is understanding its origins. Who/what made you feel inadequate, unloved, insecure? You need to begin to explore and examine these questions in order to open the way for your inner child's dynamic emergence.

This list may help you begin to sort out the origins of your present needs and emotions:

CRITICAL PARENTS

If you had parents who were overly critical and set high standards, it is likely that you have a deep sense of 'I am not good enough' and failure. You will either be a perfectionist, or 'frozen' — unable to take action and explore. There will also be a strong tendency to be Self critical.

ABUSIVE CARERS

Many of us have been the victims of verbal, physical and sexual abuse, either by someone within the family, by a carer or a complete stranger. Abuse is known to leave deep mental scars. The emotions connected with this deeply deprived act are complex and far reaching. If you are the victim of any form of physical abuse, you may find yourself suffering from unresolved anger, low Self esteem, depression, a desperate need for control, a fundamental lack of trust towards anyone who enters your space.

PARENTAL NEGLECT

We have all done it at one time or another — become preoccupied with our work, ourselves, our lives. When we are parents we often do this at the expense of our children. We are risking our child's sense of happiness. If you were the victim of workaholic parents, or parents who just never seemed to have time to give you the love and attention you needed as a child, it is more than likely you may have a sense of low Self esteem and loneliness.

PARENTAL REJECTION

One day while on holiday I heard a six year old girl ask: 'Mummy did you want me'? The mother looked stunned and reassured her she did. The girl persisted: 'Mummy you don't think I ruined your life by being born'? The mother reassured her once again.

If a child is not wanted, whether that message is verbally conveyed or not, that child will automatically know. A child who is not wanted is one who will doubt her very right to exist. This child will have a deep feeling of being unloved, rejected and will tend to never feel good enough.

PARENTAL LOSS

I had a workshop participant who was extremely overweight. Her doctors warned her that she needed to lose at least six stones or she was heading for trouble. The problem was, that Sandra was addicted to food. She couldn't stop eating. Her eating was triggered by feelings of loneliness, hopelessness, and despair in her life. When these feelings visited her she felt frozen, food became the comfort that made her feel better. When she came to my workshop we found out that her eating was related to the death of her mother. Her mother died when she was sixteen leaving her alone to bring herself up. She substituted the comfort and support her mother would have given her with food.

Loss of a parent whether it is through a death, or separation can leave us feeling very lonely and insecure. It can lead our inner child to addictions, drugs, food, seeking the love of another person.

Looking at the pain is okay. You need not feel guilty for admitting you have been hurt in the past, in doing so you are blaming no one. Your parents did the best they could with the resources they had at the time. You are taking responsibility for what happens to you now and for the future.

ORIGINAL PAIN MEDITATION

As a child I was sexually abused by a carer. I did not remember this until I had my first teenage sexual experience. It was not until then that I came to understand why my early childhood years were a total blank. My mind had safeguarded me from the pain but had not erased it.

Many of us cannot remember the pain that motivates our toxic behaviour. We have become protected by the mind but the damage is still there in the form of un-charged energy. Until your original pain is located and discharged you will continue to re-enact its destructive cycle every day in your life.

The original pain meditation has been designed just for this purpose.

You will need thirty minutes for this exercise. Read it through first before you attempt to do it. If you can, record it on a tape.

Take a few deep breaths. Inhale and exhale. Allow your mind to become centred and focused.

Starting with the top of your head and working your way down to the tips of your toes, do the muscle by muscle relaxation technique you learnt in Chapter

Healing the Inner Child

You are now in a deep state of inner relaxation. Continue to softly inhale and exhale through your nose. Visualise yourself as a small child walking down a dark corridor. This corridor represents all your fear, pain, hurt and anger. The corridor is very long, dark and narrow. It is the bridge that links you back to the past. Walk down it and allow yourself to experience the emotions and needs that resurface. Do not try to control or try to repress them.

As you near the end of the corridor you see a large wooden door with a handle. Tiptoe to reach it. Turn the handle. The door is now open. Enter into the scene before you. It is the scene of your original pain. Become one with the scene. Relive it. Notice: how old you are, who you are with, what is happening to you, how you are feeling. If you are feeling scared, lonely, hurt, angry just allow these feelings to surface and be. If you see only darkness ask Spirit to guide you back to the place you need to revisit. It is important that you do not hurry this section, allow Spirit to guide you.

When you are ready, you see yet another door. Open it and go through. You are in a luscious green forest. Inhale its wonderful aromas. Enjoy the feeling of the warm grass beneath your feet. Walk and explore the forest. Play freely. Lose yourself in abandonment for a moment.

After some time you notice a woman in blue standing by a clear blue lake. She is watching you and smiling. She invites you over.

You go to her. She tells you she is there to heal your pain, to cleanse you in her waters. As she is telling you these things, allow her to undress you and guide you into the healing water of the lake. Feel its gentle warmth caressing your body. As it does so you feel yourself enveloped in its healing properties. Feel all your tension begin to ease away. Enjoy this golden moment.

You are now ready to leave the lake. Step gently out. Lie on the grass. Feel the golden rays of the sun dry your body. You are feeling very light, very refreshed and very invigorated. You are filled with an overwhelming sense of happiness. Enjoy.

When you are ready, bid the lady in blue farewell. Your eyelids grow lighter, lighter and lighter until they now begin to open. Write your journey experience down.

Spirit first revealed this meditation to me when I was working with a group of young women who had been excluded from school. There was one particular girl who was extremely shy and suffering from a large dose of low Self esteem. When I tried to get her to examine who or what had made her feel the way she did, she did not know. In fact she believed she had been born shy. At that point I got her to close her eyes, inhale and exhale until she was deeply relaxed. As I was taking her into a deep state of relaxation I panicked when I realised the meditation I had intended to use with her was not the one. I asked Spirit to guide me. What I got was the meditation you have just completed.

My student had a very powerful meditation experience. Spirit always knows best. She found the source of her pain — an English teacher who insisted on consistently marking her work down and calling her derogatory names that questioned her intellectual capabilities.

BRING OUT THE CHILD

> *God bless the child that's got his own.*
> BILLIE HOLIDAY

Children love to play, explore, inquire, make mistakes, pick themselves up and go again. If you go to any place where you can observe children in their natural environment watch them play. You will see how children love to be themselves, children who love to have fun! Children are full of energy, new ideas, and life. They have a real sense of their own inner power. Re-awaken your inner child. Return back to the unlimited divine.

To aid you in your journey are three special meditations.

The first brings out the scared, bruised inner Self. It releases her from past traumas and returns her back to her natural creative state of happiness and dynamic potential.

The second is a meditation that came to me recently from my guiding ancestor Rashke Meneke as

I facilitated a meditation workshop at Summer Spirit: A U.K.-wide all sisters empowerment weekend. Called Power it aims to remedy feelings of inadequacy, low Self esteem and lack of Self worth.

The third releases Spirit from the trauma of those old negative behaviour patterns we tend to repeat over and over again.

Before attempting any of the meditations, read them through, contemplate them and if you can record them on tape.

HEALING FOREST

You will recognise aspects of this meditation from the Original Pain meditation you did earlier. You will need thirty minutes of quiet time.

Sit in a comfortable chair or lie on the floor. Inhale and exhale.

Using the muscle by muscle relaxation technique, relax every muscle and nerve in your body. Start from the crown of the head and work down to your toes.

When you are sufficiently relaxed, begin your visualisation.

You are a small child walking down a very long, dark corridor. This corridor represents all the hurt, trauma, pain of your inner child. Allow yourself to experience the emotions and feelings which begin to surface. Do not try to suppress them. Embrace them and allow the pain to begin its healing. You are now approaching the end of the darkness. You see a large wooded door with a large brass handle. Tiptoe and turn the handle revealing a green luscious forest. It beckons you in. You step in and enter.

Feel the soft green grass under your bare feet. Inhale the scent of mangoes, oranges, pears, bananas, nectarines, dew plums. Observe the dynamic natural spectrum of colours, plant and animal life. Take it all in. See these things as if you are seeing them for the very first time. You feel inquisitive and want to explore. Follow your intuition. Go and taste the fruits, smell the flowers. Go and be free.

As you journey through the forest you feel freer, and freer. An exquisite sense of abandonment comes over you. You hop, skip, run, laugh, play games. A voice beckons you. You immediately venture to its source. In the forest clearing you see a beautiful black woman dressed all in blue. She is standing by a clear blue lapping lake. She invites you to enter its healing waters.

You step into the warm salt water and feel a tremendous wave of inner peace wash over you. Every nerve, cell, and muscle in your body begins to feel regenerated, reinvigorated and alive. Your companion begins to sing you a healing lullaby which immediately takes you into an even deeper healing state of relaxation. Any pain, sadness, loneliness, depression you may have felt in the past now releases its hold and slips away into the depths of the lake. You feel deeply relaxed and calm. Just enjoy this precious moment.

Your companion makes you know it is time to come out of the lake. She lays you on mother earth's grass to dry under the warm golden sun. Feel its rays caressing your skin. You feel loved, nurtured and whole. Allow those same rays to enter your body, starting from the top of your head and working their way all the way down to your toes. As they do so you become filled with a magnificent white light. This white light is your divine intelligence shining forth. Embrace it. Enjoy it.

When you are ready you rise from the grass. As you do so you see a present resting by the spot. Pick it up. Unwrap it. See what it is. There is a blessing in there you need to see, hear, feel, to aid you on your way. It is a gift from Spirit which will help to guide you in your new beginnings. For some workshop participants, the gift has been a butterfly, others, affirming statements. One workshop participant received a bracelet from her deceased grandmother.

INHALE. EXHALE. It is time to return home now. Your eyelids grow lighter and lighter until they open. You are now feeling refreshed, re-invigorated and whole. Give yourself a big hug, and mentally affirm to Self 'I am whole and healed from this moment on'.
Write your experience, thoughts, insights, feelings and emotions down in your spiritual journal.

POWER
Within each and every one resides the divine intelligence that created the world. Do this powerful meditation and embrace your divine.

Put aside thirty minutes of your time and prepare your meditation space.

Let's begin.

INHALE AND EXHALE. When you feel ready do the muscle by muscle relaxation technique. Work your way down from the top of your head all the way to the tips of your toes.

You are now in a deep state of relaxation. Deepen it with a few more in-breaths and a few more out-breaths. Do not resist the power of the tranquillity that begins to embrace you. Do not hurry the feeling you are experiencing. Allow your mind to gently focus inward and your being to re-connect back to centre. Rest in the moment and enjoy.

When you are ready take these words into your trance and contemplate them.

You are feeling so wonderful. You are feeling so centred. You are feeling so beautiful. You are feeling so unique. This feeling is not just another blissful moment it is your moment to have forever. No one can take it away from you. Only the universe takes and only the universe gives you what is yours.

Someone may have told you that you are ugly, that you are no good, that you are not good enough. That same person may have also said you are not gifted or unique. They may have made you feel that you have no power. That all this power people are telling you you possess, is a myth. How can it be true, you don't feel powerful, wonderful or special. But it is true. Aren't you feeling it right now — the power? Aren't you feeling it right now — that you were made in the likeness of a divine creator? Aren't you feeling it right now — that you are a unique child of God?

The person who told you otherwise is someone, like yourself, who did not understand that they too are unique, loveable and special. That they like you are a gift from the universe. They cannot take away your power, in the same way they cannot make the sky disappear or the sun stop radiating light.

As you inhale and exhale:
Breath in Power. Breath out pain.
Breath in Power. Breath out anger.
Breath in Power. Breath out sadness.
Breath in Power. Breath out loneliness.
Breath in Power. Breath out depression.
Breath in Power. Breath out feelings of
inadequacies.
Breath in Power. Breath out Self hatred.
Breath in Power. Breath out all the hurtful,
painful things you have been told to believe
about yourself.

When you breathe in Power, really breathe it in. As you breathe, exhale breath out all the negative conditioning. Really breathe them out and let them go. Feel yourself expanding into the universe. Breath with passion. Breath like you mean it.

On each inhalation continue to breathe in Power. As you do so feel yourself growing warmer and warmer as you re-connect back to original centre. Let the celebratory warmth turn into a wonderful affirming heat. Stand up. Breath in Power, stretch your hands to the sky and feel the power entering through your palms and travelling into and through your body. Breath out the Pain, let it all go, as you do so allow your arms to fall gently by your side. Breath in Power, raise your hands to the sky again. Continue this cycle until your spirit feels blissfully fulfilled.

In your own time and when you feel ready — lie down, kneel on the floor, or remain standing, do whatever your spirit wants you to do. Enjoy the wonderful feeling that has washed over you. Allow it to sink deep into your spiritual subconscious. embrace it and know it will never go away.

As you take this new in-sperience into your being give yourself a tight hug and repeat these affirming words: 'I love myself, I love myself, I love myself, I love myself'. Repeat them mentally to Self. Now say them out aloud. send them out for universe to hear. When universe hears your affirmation, it affirms your life with love tenfold.

UNSTICKING THE GROOVE

Have you ever wondered why you keep on doing the ole' same thing over and over again without meaning to. Why that unwanted behaviour pattern, whether it be shyness, fear, anger, keeps on rearing it's ugly head when you least want it to. Maybe its because you are stuck in a groove. Every life experience you have ever had is stored in your universal spiritual memory bank. By now you know Spirit forgets nothing. It holds the blue print to all your past experiences. Whether you remember them or not, Spirit knows they are there and will keep on repeating them until you give it another way.

Lucky for us divine consciousness thought of everything when it made the world. There are no needs that are not met. All your needs were pre-known before you came out of your mother's womb. So the good news is — there is a way you can get out of that ole' tired groove. All you have to do is breathe. Breath is your on-line connection to Spirit, and visualisation is its programming tool. With breath and visualisation together there is no groove you need stay stuck in. Universe says' breathe and visualise your Self new'.

The following meditation is an extremely powerful one I adapted from my spiritual master. It is guaranteed to release your inner child from unwanted 'stuck' behaviour. Practice this exercise for forty-five minutes daily over the next four weeks or more if you need to and reap the dynamic benefits.

Review your notes for this chapter. What are the issues that have arisen for you? Maybe you have discovered you are insecure, angry, jealous, shy, anxious. Whatever the emotion take one that you are ready to release. One that has really kept you stuck in a mental, physical and spiritual rut. Think carefully of one or two typical scenarios of when that emotion makes itself known. I discovered I panic when faced with new life challenges. This behaviour stems from a bad experience I had of changing schools. I moved from one school based in the Caribbean where I was well loved, nurtured, and respected to another all white convent school based London where I felt culturally alienated and misunderstood. Write the negative scenarios down in as much detail as you can manage.

How would you like to react when you next encounter the same life scenarios? So instead of acting shy when you meet new people you may want to be more assertive and outgoing. Write down your new growth scenario in detail. Make it real.

You are now ready to meditate. Inhale and exhale. After fifteen minutes relive your first two scenarios. See the colours, hear the sounds, smell the aromas, taste the taste. Live it as if it is real. Let Spirit re-live that old behaviour pattern.

You will now relive your second scenario and feed Spirit with a new more expansive way to be.

When you are finished you feel your eyelids becoming lighter and lighter until they now open. Give yourself a big hug. Mentally affirm to Self: 'Today I love the whole of me for who I am'.

It is important to observe changes to your behaviour over the next few weeks. Write your observations and meditation insights down in your spiritual journal.

Every Black woman in America lives her life somewhere along a wide curve of ancient and unexpressed anger.

AUDRE LORDE

TO SLEEP WITH ANGER
As you've been journeying with your inner child through the pain you may have felt something hot

burning your insides. Something hot like pepper. Something hot that looks like anger. The anger may be towards a parent, carer, partner or experience. If you don't act anger out, you act it in. un dealt with anger will knot up your stomach, tie your throat, ruin your liver, grow fibroids and cyst in your womb. Anger will destroy your life and block your blessings. As John Bradshaw explains unexpressed anger is like an 'electrical storm' circulating your system. Imagine having a hurricane raging inside of you and trying to lead a balanced, harmonious, life at the same time! Make a commitment act your anger out. That doesn't mean act it out on a loved one. It means — get it out of your life!

Make peace with your anger and learn how to forgive. Bring forgiveness in your life and peace into your universal space. Forgive and release your mother, your father, your abuser, your ex-lover. Forgiveness is hard but it is a small price to pay for inner peace. I know. Forgiveness was something I found hard to do until I went on Face to Face, a dynamic empowerment workshop taught by Jackee Holder. Everything was going swell until we got to the task of forgiveness. I was resistant. How was forgiving anyone going to change my life? In fact I had no one to forgive — or so I thought. I did the exercise with half a heart and found myself pleasantly surprised. Not only did I have people to forgive. It made me feel enlightened to forgive. I thank Jackee for such a light giving experience.

This forgiveness exercise is an adaptation from

those found in Iyanla Vanzant's: Tapping The Power, A course in Miracles and Stephen Levine's Healing Into Life

This is my holy moment of release
To begin:

On one side of a lined sheet of paper, write on each line
   I forgive _____ *(the name of the person)*
   unconditionally.

Do not force yourself to think of a name. Trust your inner consciousness to guide you. It is common for the same name to come up more than once.

On the other side of your paper write on each line
   I forgive _____ *(your name)*
   unconditionally.

Once you have completed this exercise, fold the paper with the names up. Take a few silent moments to ask Spirit how it wants to dispose of it. It may be by burning and sprinkling on the land, cutting up and putting in the rubbish bin. Whatever the means, allow yourself to release the names with love. Mentally affirm to Self: *This is my holy moment of release.*

Now close your eyes. It is time to take your forgiveness into meditation.

Take a few moments to softly inhale and exhale.

When you feel the signs of trance allow Spirit to send to you someone you need to forgive. Glance on that person with a soft heart. Look on them with no judgement. If you feel any form of resistance soften it with love. See yourself forgiving the person. Do not hurry your forgiveness, take your time. Tell them you forgive them for the past or present wrongs they have done to you. Let them know you are releasing them from your life once and for all. You are re-claiming back your power. Transfer light onto them. See that person becoming happier and happier in the universal rays you are sending. See the light transforming them into beauty. As this happens begin to feel your own Self being engulfed in the radiant healing love of the universe and growing more beautiful. When you are ready release this person with love into a white light bid them farewell.

Allow more people to enter your sphere of conscious awareness and one by one you forgive them in the same way as the first and release them into the universal light of love.

When you have finished forgiving. You now forgive yourself. If you feel resistance to the idea of Self forgiveness, soften it with love. Know that it is okay to love yourself, to release the guilt, pain, or hurt you may be feeling. Know that you were not responsible for the things that hurt or bruised you in the past or present. See yourself as a child bathed in a healing white light. Hug your inner child and make her know that everything is now okay that she is now released from her suffering. As you affirm your child with love see her grow into the new beautiful adult you. Bath yourself with light. Enjoy this light experience for this is your moment of release.

When you are ready bid all those you have forgiven farewell.

Open your eyes and embrace yourself lovingly. Mentally repeat whatever affirmation Spirit gives you at this moment.

Do this exercise every day for fourteen days and longer if you need to. Write down your emotions, thoughts, insights and observations.

OTHER WAYS TO DEAL WITH ANGER

Anger is a healthy emotion, that let's you know your rights have been violated. It becomes destructive when it is not dealt with in the right manner.

Next time you are angry at a person or situation:

Take time out. Spend a few minutes with breath and in silent contemplation. When you are in trance relive the scenario in your mind. Tune into what it is that made you angry. Maybe you weren't being listened to or you felt someone had crossed a personal boundary. Often when we are angry there is a need we feel has not been met. Look deep within and find out if this need is one that you must fulfil for Self. If your anger resulted because you did not feel listened to, commit to some Self first loving and then approach the person who is the source of your current anger.

Before approaching the person who has made

you angry write down what it is you would like to say to them. I am angry with you because... If they refuse to hear you out write them a letter and post it. If you do not feel comfortable with posting it, write it anyway and keep it. The most important thing is to discharge your anger in a constructive way and let it go.

THE QUICK ROAD TO AMEN

There are times when you feel frozen by anger. In these moments you are too filled with too much rage to think logically, or even breathe. But breath is what you need.

Czar Czen breathing is the meditation I call the quick road to Amen. I have found its sequence of short in-breaths and out-breaths an excellent method for dispelling my own rage at moments when I cannot do the long inhalations and exhalations normally required for meditation. Try it yourself and feel its benefits. This meditation can be done at any time you wish to achieve a total state of inner bliss. What the ancient Egyptian's called Amen. It's better than good sex believe me!

Prepare your meditation space as normal. Fifteen to thirty minutes for this exercise is sufficient.

Your inhalation will consist of two short abdominal in-breaths. On the second breath your abdomen will be come fully extended with air.

So your inhalation sequence will go like this:

Breath in a little. Pause for a second.
Breath in a little more. Do not pause. Begin your
exhaling sequence

Your exhalation will consist of Four short
abdominal out-breaths. On the fourth breath your
stomach will be fully contracted and all the air
expelled.

Your exhalation sequence is as follows:

Breath out a little. Pause
Breath out a little more. Pause
Breath out a little more. Pause
Breath out a little more. Pause

This completes one cycle of breathing. Begin from
the top again.

NURTURING YOUR CHILD

*All kids need is a little help, a little hope and somebody
who believes in them.*

EARVIN 'MAGIC' JOHNSON

In order to grow a child needs love Your inner child is
no different. She needs all the strokes, cuddles and
kisses you can give her. She needs to know it is okay
to be herself. To touch, explore and expand.

To continue healing and nurturing your divine
child you may want to follow some of these rules. See
if you can add some of your own.

133

PERMISSION TO BE YOURSELF

I have a very good friend who was abandoned by her parents when she was four years old. At the age of thirty-eight she is a graceful, incredibly stunning and talented woman. On the surface she looks 'all put together', but underneath she is 'stuck'. She has a chronic case of low Self esteem. She feels that there is no way anyone will love and respect her for the whole of who she is. So she makes people love her and has become the forever willing helper. If you want anything doing, she's your woman. She is always there for you, don't matter what the time of day.

If you were not told how wonderful, unique and special you were as a child there is a big chance that you will feel that you, as you stand, are not good enough. You will most probably observe you have adopted a personality you feel renders you more loveable and acceptable. If this is the case your inner child is in desperate needs to know she has permission to unconditionally be herself. You need to give her lots and lots of hug and nurturing so she can know she is acceptable and loveable for who she is and just as God made her. She is unique.

FEELING THE FEELINGS

Giving your divine child permission to be herself means letting her know it's okay to feel what she is feeling. There is no right or wrong behind your feelings. Feelings just are. You have the right to feel what you are feeling. It is your reality. No one has the right to dismiss or suppress it.

Learn to get in touch with your feelings. Understand what it is you are needing when you are feeling fear, anger, loneliness, depression, frustration. The following exercise has been designed to get even the most numbed of us in touch with the need behind the feeling. It can be done at any time of your life when you experience an emotion you are unsure of — you may be feeling sad and not understand why etc.

Put aside 15-20 minutes daily over the next week.

For each day you will re-construct a different feelings scenario where you look at an emotion you want to connect with deal. Pick a different emotion for each day of the week. Write down a detail scenario for each. On day one you will take your first emotion and relive the feeling scenario you have constructed. As you relive your scenario ask yourself the question: 'what is the need behind what I am feeling'. Record your discovery. Repeat this till the last scenario. At the end of each session mentally affirm to Self: 'It's okay to feel what I am feeling.'

EXPLORING THE FREEDOM

*In every human breast, God has implanted a Principle,
which we call Love of Freedom.*

PHILLIS WHEATLEY

It is your inner child's natural instinct to be free. Freedom allows your creative potential to flow. When you lose your sense of freedom you lose touch with who you are. To expand and make the re-connection:

Do something creative — join a self-development class

Extend your comfort zone — do something you have always feared to do for fear of losing control or looking ridiculous.

Play. Playing is therapeutic. While researching this chapter I found myself, by pure coincidence — if there is such a thing! in a children's play park with my friend's children. I went on a see-saw, round-a-bout, swings for the first time in twenty years! After hours of swinging, see-sawing, and playing games I felt a new sense of inner freeness. I made a vow to Self never to lose it. I now to go to the play park once every month and let my inner child out to play.

TOUCH

Research has shown that without loving touches a new born child will die. Your inner child needs you to stroke, kiss and caress her. From small children learn it is wrong to touch themselves. Little girls are told not to touch their vaginas and little boys their penis. Touch becomes taboo. Become comfortable with your own touch:

Stand naked in front of a full length mirror. Look lovingly at every part of your body starting from your head down to your toes. Now Allow your hands to stroke your forehead. Say quietly and gently to yourself: 'I love you forehead'. From your forehead work your way down to your eyes, your nose, your cheeks, lips, chin, ears, neck, shoulders, breast and so on until you reach your toes.

Give yourself a big hug. Affirm mentally to Self: 'I love and accept myself for the whole of who I am'

Do this exercise anytime you need some Self first loving.

TIME

If your inner child has learnt it is not okay to be herself, then she has also learnt she does not have the right to her own time. Begin to create 'Down Time' just for you and Self. Putting time aside for Self proclaims to the world: 'I am a worthy. I am valuable. I am a creation of the universe'

Here is a suggestion list of nurturing things to do in your Down Time:
1. Take a warm aromatherapy/bubble bath.
2. Read an inspirational book.
3. Go for a sauna.
4. Go for a massage.
5. See a good movie.
6. Go window shopping.
7. paint, draw or write a poem.
8. Listen to some inspirational music.
9. Eat out at your favourite restaurant by yourself.
10. Visit an art gallery or another place of interest
11. Go for a walk.
12. Go to the gym or a keep fit class.
13. Go see a funny play.

14. Give yourself a sensuous massage.
15. Go for that long desired break in the country side or out of the country.
16. Go for a scenic walk.
17. Feed the birds.
18. Cook a really nice meal just for yourself. Eat it by candlelight.
19. Make an affirmation tape.
20. Go have that long awaited manicure or pedicure.
21. Write a love letter to yourself.
22. Make time for your goals.
23. Write in your spiritual journal.
24. Meditate.

DREAM AGAIN

You have to give a kid a dream.

GEORGE FOREMAN

Children love to make belief. They love to dream. Dreaming is the stuff of possibilities. Possibilities tell us we can be anything, we want to be as long as we believe in it enough. Think of an actor, musician, artist, that you respect and admired. That person did not get where they are today because of luck, they got there because they dared to dream and believe in their gifts. Our fore-parents did not escape the devastating chains of slavery by chance — they dreamed of freedom. Through their belief in their dream they made their emancipation and ours a possibility. What do we call people of great achievers? Don't we call them great visionaries? People with unlimited vision.

Without vision we die. When a person has given up hope in their own uniqueness, don't you say: 'She needs to learn to dream again.' Dreaming allows expansion. It aligns us with the creative gifts God has given us.

Our elders tell us, each and every person has come into this world with a unique divine purpose. You reading this book have something special to give the world. You have journeyed into this life-time with a gift. You are an earthly vessel overflowing with infinite abundance. Neglecting your talents is to opt to live empty, unfulfilled lives. When you're not doing what you love doing, how do you feel? Don't you feel low, depressed, adrift, miserable? Don't you feel like you just can't go on anymore? These feelings are Gods way of letting you know 'Girlfriend you're not doing your thang.' You're not doing what you were sent into this world to do, until that time — you will keep on feeling those feelings.

Being tuned in with Divine Purpose is to be on-line with the Wealth Supply of universe. Doing and trusting in your God given abilities allows heaven to open her doors. With Universe on your side you are left wanting for nothing. You become the dynamic embodiment of the potency of giving and receiving. To accept life's blessings is to receive, with an open loving heart — God's trust in your abilities to make the world a happy place. To use your vision is to give back to your fellow man, Self and universe. Life is an open stream of giving and receiving. Failing to be in the flow is to choose spiritual death.

For years, after graduating from the School of Oriental and African Studies, London University, I could not decide on a career path. I loved writing and as a result I wanted to be a Journalist. I also loved the world of holistic healing. The two did not seem to mix. So I pursued my 'first' love — writing. I freelanced for a few national black magazines and newspapers. I enjoyed writing and got paid for it, but deep down I felt unfulfilled. Something was missing from my life — my unique life purpose.

It was not until after the birth of my son that I decided to let go and let universe in. For once in my life I was going to give up resistance and go with God's plan. It was frightening, but I did it — this is the place I ended up: writing this book, teaching meditation and empowerment to the community. I always express my surprise, to people, at the work universe choose for me to do.

Learning to trust is to tap into the abundant pool of universe. God has a divine plan for you, as he had for me. Your inner child needs to know this. You need to help her let go of resistance and teach her to trust again. Early on, as a child she put her trust out there only to quickly withdraw it. Through abusive adults and negligent carers she discovered — the world isn't a safe place after all. To trust is to embrace Universal Truth. Universal Truth states that everything is real. You are real, God is real, Your gifts are real. In other words it is an acceptance of the belief — My reality is what I can see, as well as, what I cannot see. When what you can't see becomes part of your world again — all that God is waiting to offer you can be received.

If your inner child has lost touch with her gifts do this simple exercise

Close your eyes and take a few slow inhalations and exhalations.

Without thinking write down on a blank sheet of paper three things you wanted to be in your life.

Circle the first profession that appears at the top of your list. From my numerous experience of doing this exercise in my workshop, I have discovered, if it wasn't for fear the antithesis to trust, the first thing that appears at the top of our list is the career or talent the individual would be pursuing in their life.

Another insightful life purpose exercise is one I discovered in Live Your Dreams by Les Brown, an inspirational African-American Motivational speaker. It is one I have used, in my workshops often, with brilliant results.

Imagine you have died today

Write your obituary on a blank sheet of paper. Imagine you are somebody else writing about your life qualities and achievements

Read your obituary back to yourself. Take note of the things you discover about yourself. What are the things you would have liked to have achieved or done in your life if you had not died today — write them down.

Using your favourite affirmation book obtain an affirming statement to support you in your new visioning. One workshop participant received the following from Black Pearls by Eric V Copage: 'I used to want the words 'She tried' on my tombstone. Now I want 'she did'

The results from this exercise are always without fail very powerful. Most people end up in tears on the realisation they have not used their life gifts. There are those, like one workshop participant I remember, who realised they had been using their gift all along!

VISIONING MEDITATION

> *Shoot for the moon.*
> *Even if you miss you will land among the stars.*
>
> LES BROWN

Your visioning can be as wild as you want it to be. Don't hold back, allow your mind to wander and explore life's endless offerings. You can be anything the Divine Intelligence has Willed you to be. All you have to do is believe. Your unique gifts are yours to give to the world. Trust in them, claim them, believe in them — they are the presents bestowed by consciousness for your happiness. God has given everything you need to create bliss in this lifetime, and well into your next. Use them, they have been given with an open loving heart.

Dream as large as you want. You are an expansive being of the universe.

Prepare your meditation space, as normal.

Write down on a piece of paper the thing/s you would love to be achieving with your life right now and for the future. As you are writing do not hold back. Passively observe what Spirit chooses for you to put down.

Look back over what you have written.

When you are ready close your eyes and begin to softly inhale and exhale for fifteen minutes. After the specified time see yourself in your new role. Do this for up to fifteen minutes or longer if you desire.

Whatever comes to you in your meditation, do not put up any resistance, do not limit the possibility for expansion.

EARTHLY STEPS

You have now sown what you want to reap into Spirit. Spirit is the 'Great Doer' will help you achieve these goals as you take your earthly steps to energise them.

Here is a list of earthly things you can do to help you realise your unique life purpose:

Look at the qualifications and training the vision requires. What don't you have that is holding you back? It may be that you need to do some art classes or do a short course in human biology. Whatever it is that your vision needs for it to work write it down on a sheet of paper. Don't despair if your list looks daunting. Prioritise one or two things you can start with now.

Go to the library, bookshop. Have some fun and do your research.

Speak to people who are fulfilling their life purpose, ask them their background and how they made it. Particularly talk to those who are working in the area you wish to be in.

Read inspirational and uplifting autobiographies

Bear in mind it is never too late to re-discover what God has given to you.

Stick loving and supporting statements up in key areas of your living space: above your work station, bathroom sink, bed, kitchen work top.

Pray and ask for guidance and help.

FEAR

Life has frightened me now and then, and if I've shown uncommon bravery, I've failed to notice it.

GORDON PARKS

Fear is something that holds most of us back from doing what we need to be doing. Here are a few things to help you through the fear:

There is not a moment of your day when universe does not support you, all you have to do is reach out and ask your inner consciousness for help. This can be done through, prayer, libation, meditating in silent communion with God.

Healing the Inner Child

Fear is the antithesis of trust. Learning to trust eases the anxiety and panic you may often feel when starting a new venture. Trust starts from the belief you are one with the unlimited creative potential of universe.

Examine what is going on when you feel fearful. Do the Feel The Feelings meditation you did earlier in this chapter. Know that wherever your fear comes from belongs to the past — you are now claiming responsibility for your future.

Do the Visioning meditation often. This will replace old fearful programming from the past with your new expansive dreams for the future.

Use loving and supportive affirmations often.

A liberating truth is, that fear never goes away 100 per cent so follow empowerment trainer, Susan Jeffer's advise: 'Feel The Fear and do it anyway'

VISIONING STATEMENTS

> *All God's chillun got wings.*
> SPIRITUAL

> *Bringing the gifts that my ancestors gave*
> *I am the dream and the hope of the slave.*
> *I rise.*
> *I rise.*
> *I rise.*
> MAYA ANGELOU

I'm the greatest.
MUHAMMAD ALI

Keep hope alive.
JESSE JACKSON

I've always known I was gifted, which is not the easiest thing in the world for a person to know, because you're not responsible for your gift, only what you do with it.
HAZEL SCOTT

We are positively a unique people. Breathtaking people. Anything we do, we do big!
LEONTYNE PRICE

Keep your eyes on the prize.
FREEDOM SONG

It's a gift with me hearing music the way I do. I don't know where it comes from, it's just there. I don't question it.
MILES DAVIS

A mind is a terrible thing to waste.
UNITED NEGRO COLLEGE FUND

Healing the Inner Child

*Only leadership — that intangible combination of gifts,
discipline, information, circumstance, courage, timing,
will and divine inspiration — can lead us out of the crisis
in which we find ourselves.*
JESSE JACKSON

*The past is a ghost, the future a dream,
and all we ever have is right now.*
BILL COSBY

Where there is no vision, the people perish.
JAMES BALDWIN

*The dream is real, my friends.
The failure to make it works the unreality.*
TONI CADE BAMBARA

*I don't know what the future may hold, but I know who
holds the future.*
REVEREND RALPH ABERNATHY

*tI submit to you that if a man hasn't discovered something
that he will die for, he isn't fit to live!*
MARTIN LUTHER KING JR

*Surround yourself with only people who are going to lift
you higher.*
OPRAH WINFREY

I have learned that success is to be measured not so much by the position that one has reached in life as by the obstacles which he has overcome while trying to succeed.
BOOKER T WASHINGTON

I think that the human race does command its own destiny and that destiny can eventually embrace the starts.
LORRAINE HANSBERRY

Up You mighty race, you can accomplish what you will.
MARCUS GARVEY

Every people should be the originators of their own destiny, the projectors of their own schemes, and the creators of the events that lead their destiny — the consummation of their own desires.
MARTIN DELANY

The greatness of peoples springs from their ability to grasp the grand conceptions of being. It is the absorption of a people, of a nation, of a race, in large majestic and abiding things which lifts them up to the skies.
ALEXANDER CRUMMELL

Healing the Inner Child

*The real answer to race problems in this country is
education. Not burning and killing. Be ready, Be qualified.
Own something Be somebody. That's Black Power.*
JAMES BROWN

Grow in your own patch. Stay put and blossom.
NTOZAKE SHANGE

*I believe that dreams do come true. Often they might not
come when you want them. They come in their own time.*
DIANA ROSS

We had been too long out of the light. It was our time.
BERNICE JOHNSON REAGON

Have a vision. Be demanding.
COLIN POWELL

*I stood up in front of a speech class and said,
'I plan to make my living with my oratory skills, and I'd
like to be a talk show host.' There was a pause, then the
most incredible laughter you've ever heard in your life.*
ARSENIO HALL

Everyone is more or less the master of his own fate.
THE TRAVELLER AND FORTUNE

> *I had to practically hypnotise myself into thinking I was*
> *going to be successful.*
> **JOHN SINGLETON**

6: AWAKENING THE GODDESS

She is a friend to my mind. She gathers me. The pieces I
am, she gathers them and gives them back to me
in all the right order.

TONI MORRISON

It started of as a small whisper and rose to the air like thunder. 'Phat Bambalasam, Nego fram Bambalasam...' The priestess stretched elegantly and gracefully to the four corners of the earth, spinning and weaving universe's primal energy back and forth into the mother's womb centre. I started to rock, and hold the ancestors four month unborn child in my stomach. The sixty or so women who had gathered in the Auset's sacred healing circle began to sway. We chanted in unison to cleanse whatever bad vibes we were holding in our hearts.

The cool air grew warmer as the God's responded to our invocation for them to unify and make our auras whole. 'Phat Bambalasam, Nego fram Bambalasam'. The chant grew louder. The priestess stomped in time with the rhythm. The cleansing heat began. It started at the base of my spine, uncoiling like a snake it flickered to the top curving into every cell, muscle and sinew of my body. It was an awesome experience. There I stood bathed in the ancient universal light. In the company of my sisters my healing began.

On the back of Elegba, 'the Divine Messenger of

the Gods, opener of the way', Auset, The Great Mother, came out from the surrounding bushes dressed in blue silk, moonstones, cowry shelled head-dress — this is how my vision beheld her. Graceful, powerful she stepped into our midst with her cool watery presence. She was on a mission. A mission to heal. To right our ailing hearts. To re-harmonise our out of sync energies. To focus our attention back to the place of our centre. She could do all of this and more, because she was all of our great potential awaiting release.

Her soft sweet words began to unravel our pain. They poured water onto our defensive fires.

'The fire, the fire,' she sighed and continued 'too much fire my children. Too much. Where is the river, where is the ocean, where is the water? The healing water of life. Where is it? Is it in the fire you hold in your heart? Is it in the fire you hold in your womb? Is it in the fire you hold as your defence, your shield? Where is it? I can't find it. The Great Mother cannot see the water in your life. The Great Mother cannot see the cool place of your centre. The Great Mother cannot find the feminine principle that will help you to heal your life. That will help you to heal your wounds. That will help you to heal your sorrows. That will help you to heal your fertility problems of mind, body and soul. The mother is searching and yet I cannot find what needs to be gestating in your life — in the life of a woman. Let your life essence flow. Let it flow and heal you. Let it flow and make you at peace. Let it flow to help you build nations of good men and women. Let it flow, let it flow, let it flow like a mighty river.'

The Mother was grieving, we were grieving as she started to heal our past and create the future. Her devotion to life was felt in our guts. We began fell into her ocean and cried. Tears are the mother's significator. They told us she her mission to piece us back together was at work. They soaked my face. Mingled with the ritual bath and jasmine oils rubbed on my body. Washed away my frustration. They washed away my worries of being pregnant with no idea of how I was going to feed the spirit child I had growing inside of me. They tore into the dark veil of my fear. They pieced me back together and made me whole.

> *I had grown big, but my mother was bigger, and that would always be so.*
> **JAMAICA KINCAID**

'Ain't no man ever going to take advantage of me'. In fact 'ain't nobody ever going to take advantage of me ever again'. Hundreds of thousands of black women around have said it. You've said it. I've said it. Our mother's have said it, and their mothers before them have. These words have passed down through the generations of black women. They make the heart grow hard, the giving less, the receiving almost non-existent. They make us empty. They make us hurt our sisters with jealousy, meanness, and plain nastiness. They make us hurt our men through not trusting again. They make us hurt our nation by no longer building on the foundation of love and respect. They make us hurt our children — we punish the boys for being who they are, and tell the girls being who they are is not okay. Most of all we hurt ourselves. We close ourselves to love. We close ourselves to sharing. We close ourselves to change. We close ourselves to growth. We close ourselves to the abundance of the universe. We close ourselves to life. We make ourselves sick on the physical plain — fibroids, cancer, ulcers, high blood pressure, the list goes on. We make ourselves sick on the mental plane — breakdowns, depression, neurosis. We make ourselves sick on the spiritual plane — dis-ease with Spirit.

When you say those words, you are telling universe what it gave you is faulty. There's something wrong with the way it created life. Why after all create women. Women are no good for nothing. Who wants to be a woman, anyway? You send universe the message you want nothing to do with what it has to offer. You let universe know you are fed up, you are going to change the natural divine order of things around. You are going to tamper with the cosmos. You are going to make your own divine laws. You tell universe the internal mechanisms of Spirit it has given you as your sole survival mechanism is no longer needed — you don't want no part of it. Not one iota. In simple terms — you tell universe to get lost.

Awakening the Goddess

Imagine a house with no foundation? I can here you say 'how on ever earth can a house have no foundation?' How indeed. It is almost unimaginable, isn't it? How can anything stand with nothing to hold it up? How can a table stand with no legs, a roof stay up without beams? How can a tree stand without roots or a bird fly without wings? It's impossible. We all know this, but when it comes to applying the law much closer to home, we suddenly change the rules — 'I don't need nobody but myself. Not no man, no sister, no child. I can cope fine being just the way I want to be hard faced and loveless.'

Don't matter how much you want to change the facts — universal law affects all of God's creatures, and that includes you. You are not exempt from God's law. You can decide to close your heart to it but you are still under its jurisdiction. The fact is God made you a woman and it ain't that bad after all. God did not give you a penis and make you a man. He did not make you androgynous either. Spoken simply — he made you a woman. He breathed the feminine principle into your nostrils for you to express it in this lifetime. He made your womanhood your survival mechanism. Your strength and foundation. Your woman hood is revered throughout the whole world. She is deified in ancient Kamit as Auset 'essence of life', West Africa as Yemanje 'Mother of All Living Things', India as Europe as Madonna and child. In our ancestral pantheon of Gods she was revered as one of the most important amongst the Gods. Without her there is no other. What does a mother do, if not

155

birth?

When you disrespect your woman hood. You are choosing to disrespect the most sacred valuable part of yourself — the Goddess within.

In the infinite world of my universe is my divine power to heal. When I tap into it, embrace it, claim it, I tap into the unlimited earth centre of my mother — the power of my Goddess within.

THE STORY OF AUSAR AND AUSET

Once upon a time in a land called Kemit, land of the Black People, a benevolent king, Ausar, ruled alongside his wife Auset, The Mother of The Essence of all Living Things. During their reign the people were happy as they lived in perfect balance and harmony with the Gods and divine law.

Needless to say the Kingdom of Ausar prospered and grew.

Seeing the wonderful prosperity within his Kingdom, Ausar decided to travel the lands of the world and spread his divine message of peace and equilibrium with all things. He set off leaving his wife in control.

The gentle Queen continued to reign with love and kindness. Disputes were settled fairly, harmonious relationships fostered between man and woman, woman and child, woman and woman, man and man.

Unbeknown to the people and the kindly Queen peace was not to reign for much longer. Set, Auset's evil brother, hated the way things were. Everything was so peaceful. He wanted chaos, fighting, lovelessness,. These were the things that made his spirit happy. He thought and thought of a way to change the order of things until he came across the perfect solution — he would have a party in honour of the returning King. He gathered 72 conspirators together. They made busy with the arrangements.

The party was good. Drinks and food flowed with abundance. Music rocked the house. The King and his wife were in excellent spirits. As the party warmed up and the people and Royal Family became even more jovial, Set suggested a game. He brought out a magnificent wooden chest beset with jewels and showed it to the room. The game — to see who could fit their entire body in the chest. The prize — the chest itself. The chest was passed around the whole room but nobody could fit their body in. Some came close. Try as they may to give themselves that extra squeeze they still could not fit into it. Then came Ausar's turn. His whole body fitted into the chest. Set had made the chest just for him. Against the uproar of the party goers, Set and his conspirators quickly nailed Ausar into the coffin and made off. The Royal guards tried to rescue their King, but Set and his evil companions were too well prepared for a fight.

Set and his men travelled a long distance before they dumped Ausar's coffin in the River Nile. On the following day Set returned home and ousted his sister, Auset, from power. He declared himself the new ruler. The Nation of Kamit along with the grieving King's wife were horrified that the peace and harmony they had worked so hard to establish was to be destroyed, by greed, corruption, murder and pillage.

The queen vowed to never rest until order had been restored and her husband's body found. After what felt like days and days of travelling and asking everyone she met if they had seen the magnificent chest — she came across a group of children who had. They told her they had seen it floating down the great Nile river. Filled with hope the grieving widow continued her search. One night as she lay her weary body to rest she dreamt of the destination of Ausar's coffin. As she was one with divine law, she knew the dream to be true.

The following day she eagerly continued her travels. Within a few days she landed at Babylos, a Port City in Southern Syria where she found the coffin as her dream had predicted.

After many days at sea Auset returned back to the land of Kamit, where Set still continued his tyrannical reign of power. Vowing to restore peace, she transformed herself into a beautiful swallow and hovered over her deceased husband, raised his phallus and received his seed. She carefully hid his body in a mangrove and went away to a safe haven to conceive their son, Heru, who would continue his mother's fight for restored harmony in the Kingdom. During the Queen's absence Set and his men had discovered Ausar's body. Outraged that it had turned back up, the evil ruler vowed to get rid of it forever. Chopping it into fourteen pieces he dispersed it all over the world. Unknown to Set a shrine to Ausar grew were each piece fell.

On giving birth to her beautiful son, Auset heard about Set's evil deed. Weeping she vowed once again to find the body of her husband. This time she enlisted the help of her sister Nebt-Het. They travelled the whole world until every single piece of the dead King was collected and reunified. To make sure Set and his evil doers could not get to him again they mummified him and buried him at the bottom of the ocean where he reigned as divine King of the Underworld.

Ausar visited his son's dreams on many occasions to remind him of his divine purpose — to restore God's law. Heru heeded the dreams. When he became old enough he began battle with his evil uncle. They fought and fought. Some battles he won, others he lost. All in all the war remained a stalemate. Until one day Heru heard about Tehuti, the ancient sage who possessed the third eye of knowing. He journeyed to the wise God's home. When he arrived he explained his mission. Happily Tehuti, gave him his eye of seeing. Set's evilness could not defeat the goodness of wisdom. Needless to say the he lost the battle. Despite his terrible deeds, Auset's heart had not hardened. She reprieved him on the condition that he became the mouth piece for righteousness throughout the world.

The words were living things to her. She sensed them bestriding the air and charging the room with strong colours.

Our elders never said anything without intent and purpose. Stories were never just stories for telling sake. They were multi-layered scientific instruments which embodied a series of universal truths. Whether it was about the human psyche or the ways of the world we live — the stories our ancestors told were imbued with meaning. The tradition of story telling still exist with us today. Just watch a group of black folks together. Look how they banter, wax lyrical and dramatically illustrate their point or principle with a story. The European conquerors who stepped foot on our ancient lands could not understand why we loved to tell a story. Their label of us as 'foolish natives' ironically reflected their own lack of divine knowing.

The story of Ausar and Auset is just one more fine example of the high understanding our forefathers and mothers had of Self. They understood the conflicts, threads, wheels and bolts of spirits workings. They knew what it took to make us angry, and what it took to bring us to hetep. They understood the whole gamut of our emotions, our needs, desires, and what place and order they occupied in the divine order of things. They were spiritual doctors.

As one of the most important religious stories of ancient Kamit the story of Ausar and Auset allows us a view the mirror of our inner workings. Ausar, Auset, Heru and Set — the four main characters — each represent an aspect of our universal archetypal make up.

AUSAR

'The Good Shepherd', 'Lord of Eternity', 'Ruler of The Dead and Lord of the Underworld'. Whatever name we choose to call him, Ausar represents wo-mans divinity on earth. He symbolises what we are when we are fully aligned with Spirit — God people. Living as a God person is to live with vision, potentiality, omnipotency and a total sense of inner peace. It is the ability to occupy the top of your tree, the way in which Ausar occupied the top of his. It is to live in the white light of universe's protection. To live in total balance and harmony with all living things. It is what our ancestors aspired to become.

Just go into any museum, go to the Egyptian section. If you can't get to the museum go buy a book on Ancient Egypt or borrow one from the library. Look at the pictures of the way the pharaohs/Shekems were buried — they were mummified with their arms crossed. In either hand they hold a crook and a flail. Now look at the image of the God Ausar. You will notice that he too is mummified with his arms crossed holding the symbol of the shepherd — the crook and the symbol for discipline — the flail. The Shekems and the whole nation of Kamit believed passionately in their own divinity. In life it was what they aspired to achieve. In death it was to that which they hoped to return.

HERU vs SET

> *The devil made me do it.*
> FLIP WILSON

It sounds good doesn't it, that we are God people. That we can choose to live a life aligned with Spirit free from worries, hassle, anger, heartache, hysteria, sorrow, crap. A life where there is nothing but peace, sweet peace and balance. But there is just one little snag, God doesn't make anything easy. He understands that for us humans to appreciate anything we have to fight for it. You've heard of all those stories, where a woman will throw herself in front of a moving car to protect her child. She would rather her life be taken than that of her own child, but why — is she crazy, has she lost her marbles, does she need to be committed to a mental home. It's simple — she gave birth to that child, fought with the morning sickness, the threatened miscarriages, the pain of giving birth, the doctors, the nurses. She fought for the safe passage of his/her life into this world.

When we fight for things we are more likely to value, respect and hold onto them. When we fight for a thing we are telling universe I want this thing so badly will you help me to get it. Will you help me keep it. As long as it is according to the Divine Will universe answers your prayers. Your inner creative potential is just the same. It is there for you to have. It is your wealth house of abundance. It is the manifestation of your unlimited essence, but you have to get pass one little thing to get to it — Set. He is where Christianity took it's concept of the devil from. Think of the devil. How is he depicted? Go to a church and have a look at the pictures. Better still go to an art gallery where they have a showing of classical European paintings. The devil is portrayed as a animal seething with red hot passion poised with a pitch fork in his hand. The devil is nothing more than what our ancestors called ego.

When you're trying to give up cream topped chocolate cakes, isn't ego there prodding you to taste that sweet, rich, yummy chocolate? Or when you're mad, isn't it like you've been pitch forked into action by a little voice telling you 'you're not going to take that are you?', 'Are you really going to let him/her get away with it?', 'You can't stay cool over this. They'll just do it again'.

Just as in the story of Ausar and Auset, where Set he conspired to kill Ausar and eventually chopped him up into 14 pieces. Ego will conspire to suffocate your attempts to bring peace, equilibrium, and inner prosperity into your life. The more you try to use your will (Heru) to change your life for the better, the more ego will be on your case. Ego wants to be where it doesn't belong — at the top of your tree. Ego hates love, joy, divine law. Give him a good old fight any day and he's happy. Unlike your indwelling intelligence, ego's intentions are far from good. Ego strives in strife. Having ego rule your life is like empowering a child to run a nation. Uhmm. I don't think any of us like the sound of that now, do we!

AUSET

No woman nuh cry.
BOB MARLEY

There is nothing like a good woman to save the day. We've all seen her with the small child who cuts his leg, or burns his hand. We've seen her with the over demanding needy husband. We've seen her in our mothers, our sisters, our friends. Above all we've seen her in ourselves. As women we are so busy fixing and piecing everyone else together we forget to fix ourselves. We forget to pamper, love, and nurture the good the Creator has given us. We forget to find time just for Self. We give so much to others that we forget how to receive. The worst thing about the whole scenario is that we really come to believe we are not deserving. We are not deserving of love, we are not deserving of affection, we are not deserving of nurturing, we are not deserving of respect. In fact we are not deserving of anything that shows us to be human like everyone else. We are strong women. The strong have no needs, isn't that the mantra we repeat. The strong can stand up for themselves. The strong don't need no support or propping up that stuff is only for weaklings. Don't we always hear our mothers say, 'I don't need no one else. I did it all by myself and so can you'. It is true our mothers often did it all alone but people still need people. People need support. People need nurturing. Just because we may be doing it all by ourselves doesn't mean that Self becomes less important. However you want to fool yourself, Self demands nurturing from the inside out. When we choose to ignore this law, we do it at our own expense.

I have a sister friend who had chosen to do just that.

Karen (not her real name), was one hell of a sister. She had a strength which I admired tremendously. She always seemed to bounce back from the worse situations. She was always in work, she was always positive, she just seemed to have it together all the time. I respected her, because my life felt like such a shambles. After graduating from university, I could not find any work. After trying for over a year to find employment in the area I desired — publishing and media, I gave up. yes I gave up on myself. I felt lost and soon had no focus or zeal for life. After a while I began to look for jobs in pizza hut, McDonald's, you name a fast food place — I've worked there. I worked long hours for shitty money. Many of the positions I walked out of. Others I just got the boot from. I could not seem to hold a job down. My frustration rocked while my Self esteem took a plummet. Karen was the friend, who by her living example of positively and bounce-back-ability, gave me the courage to go on and get a life.

There was just one thing, Karen had one problem — she felt she had to be strong all the time. Her mother had died when she was very young. Her father had booted her out of the house when she was at college studying for her media degree. All in all, Karen did not know what it was to be nurtured. All she knew was — only the strong survive. Her motto had gotten her far until one day she had a baby.

Her boyfriend was a decent guy. He worked hard, brought home the bacon. He had always shown signs of being a bit piggish. He believed men did not do things like wash up the dishes, sweep up the floor or cook their own dinners. Karen did not mind so much. She got on with it like she had always done. When they discussed having a baby, Karen was all for it. She knew her boyfriend would not help out much with the child care — it wasn't his sort of thing, but as always she felt she could cope.

God always sends us the lessons we need to learn. Sometimes they are harsh, but they are what we need at the time to see our way clear. God sent Karen a child. At first things were going well. For the first eight months she looked after her son, while her boyfriend continued to work. As she had predicted he didn't help out much, if at all, with the child care. In fact he became a child himself. Taking it for granted she was always at home, he began to leave his dirty washing for her to do. HE even stopped tidying after himself. Slowly but surely Karen became a regular commercial-ad mother — the ones you see with the baby in the right arm, the soap powder in the left, the washing machine, hoover, dishwasher all going at once in the background. Karen didn't mind her boyfriend['s lack of participation in their son's existence, she was use to just getting on with it. Things were going fine on the home front, according to Karen's idea of what fine was, until she had to return back to work.

The early hours, late nights, dirty nappies, dirty dishes, dirty laundry, demands from her work, hungry bellies to feed, not to mention her boyfriends frequent background rantings — she wasn't a good mother — after all what mother leaves her baby to cry with a wet bum, makes her man come home and wait for his meal. It was all began to get to her. She found herself despondent, constantly tearful, depressed, fatigued and eventually resentful. Despite all of this Karen still held by her motto: Only The Strong Survive. She refused to let her aunt look after her son — don't matter how many times she offered. Karen really thought if she took her aunt up on her suggestion, people would think that she could not cope. That she was an unfit mother. She even refused suggestions that she went away on holiday. As her physical, spiritual and mental health deteriorated, Karen refused to see the problem. She refused to talk to her boyfriend about taking on his fair share of the child rearing work. She refused to acknowledge that while he was out pumping iron and partying her own needs were being put to one side. Karen refused to accept that even the strong need to lean on someone.

One day after Karen had called me over a regular daily six month period, always in tears, I decided to tell her a few home truths: 'You need to sought it out', 'Get a grip', 'Look at yourself — you're a run-down mess'. I admit I was harsh to her that day, but she needed to be told. She didn't need to be cushioned her. Cushions only soften the hard floor beneath the surface. Karen needed to feel the surface she was sitting on. She needed to see her situation before it saw her out.

The last time I spoke to Karen she had just finished speaking to her counselling. She still has the boyfriend, is still tending to everyone's needs, and she hasn't stopped cooking, cleaning, scrubbing, working and looking after baby simultaneously. The difference now is that she has started the process of Self first love.

When you let go of resistance and empty strength you allow the Mother to move in and do her work. You say no to hardship, lovelessness, hate, limitation, jealously, resentment, anger and yes to a life of ease and grace. As a woman your gift from God is the gift of coolness, moistness, stillness, and easy access to inner peace. This is your uniqueness. Your strength. You are the Yin of the Yang. You are the shady side of the hill. The place where men, children, creatures and Self come to rest their weariness. You are the centre that holds the healing. You are the womb of universe's creative abundance. From you came all of God's creatures. From you came all things. God chose you to be the conception vessel of Spirit's heartbeat. In our spiritual systems you are the one who is chosen for priesthood. The ancients were far from stupid — they knew you held the waters that conducted the messages from the underworld of ancestors, Gods, and spirits.

When the Mother moves into your life the Goddess moves in and dis-ease moves out. As in the story she is the force which will bring you back from your spiritual death and piece you back together. She will mummify you and wrap you in her balm. She will make you whole. To make whole is the true meaning of healing. What is a Goddess, but a splendid, divine, powerful energy in motion. Being made whole is to come home to your magnificence. Your magnificence is not an energy outside of Self. It is not an alien being waiting to jump in and take you over like some cheap B class horror film. Your magnificence is the other side of who you are. The unseen eternity that dwells within. It is that part of you which patiently waits like a seed to grow into a tree and manifest it's beauty outwards to every part of your life.

The Mother is devoted to healing. Just look how she travelled far and wide to heal her husband — Ausar — the God symbol of your divinity. To unleash the Goddess is to unleash your own devotion to Spirit's demand for inner healing.

AWAKENING THE MOTHER

Music is one of the closet link-ups with God that we can probably experience. I think it's a common vibrating tone of the musical notes that holds all life together.

MARVIN GAYE

It was dark. The bass line was thumping. The young guy beside me was going schematic. He was busting those moves the only way a black man can. His spirit must have been in tune. There was no way he could get his arms, legs, upper torso and hips to do seemingly different things all at the same time in perfect harmony. I could feel my own body beginning to rock. My steps started of unsure and grew in confidence as the drum and base began to lick in its groove. I had never been to a Jungle rave before — the new dance craze from the streets of inner city London. When my brother was making his Jungle music documentary and going to all the clubs, I showed no intention of trailing behind him. What had changed my mind? A man of course! A man who I happened to be crazy about. Crazy enough to want to sweat in a warehouse with hundreds of black gyrating bodies.

The music continued its thumping. The DJ just got badder and the bass line harder. My body was in a pool of sweat. I couldn't stop rocking. Couldn't stop moving. The beat had me. I felt like I was in an African village dancing with Shango the God of War. I was a warrior moving calmly, surely forward to meet my enemy. The vibe of the night was good. We rockers, were spirits united together in one beat. As I sweated and moved, I suddenly understood the appeal of Jungle. It was a place for young black youths to find some healing. A healing concrete walls of an urban jungle could not offer. Through its mad but rhythmic beat, Jungle, allowed the dancer's spirit to talk out its frustrations. To punch the air, with arms, feet and torso. It allowed Spirit a voice. It allowed Spirit to let the world know I dislike where I'm at. I dislike the oppression. I dislike my potentiality being squashed. I need to be free. I need to express my unlimited creativity. I need balance. I need harmony. Then it allowed Spirit to enter its own quiet space of belonging with a sweet sigh.

The traditional relationship of healing, music and spirit is explained in an extract from The Healing Drum: African Wisdom Teachings by Yaya Diallo and Mitchall Hall:

While playing for community dancing, the Minianka musicians may sense disturbances as they manifest in people's dancing. When they amuse themselves, people reveal their serious side. As they relax, they let out their suppressed tendencies. The fact that each profession has its characteristic dance steps and movements gives valuable diagnostic indications of a person's inner balance. When a blacksmith comes to the centre of the circle, the musicians play the smith's rhythm. If he dances like a fisherman spirit, as the spirits, like humans, have their occupational specialisations. If another person rolls around no matter what kind of music is played, the nature of the spirit that has possessed him is revealed. Each spirit provokes characteristic movements, and these are described in folktales that the elders repeat. These tales convey insights and give information acquired by the ancestors.

The domain of Sikiere-folo is vast. Some

disturbances do not wait for music to come out. For example, someone goes into the bush and suddenly becomes haunted by a spirit that cries out after him. He may take off all his clothes. According to a traditional saying. 'You can hide your fool at home until the moment he walks down the street naked.' Or people suddenly explode in a rage with no warning signs.

There is no time to investigate when they were first afflicted by madness, so revealing a problem through music is no panacea.

Village musicians never advertise as healers. When we are playing and notice a dancer behaving abnormally, we keep silent about it at first and continue to observe. If we still sense the person is disturbed, we discreetly approach the family to inform them of what we have seen. We then ask them if they have noticed anything unusual and if they are aware of any conflicts in the individual's life. We extend our inquiries to others, such as members of the age group, if our fist suspicions seem to be confirmed. We report to the family on what we have learned.

it is up to the family to recognise that one of their members is becoming Sikiere-folo. T Hey will then ask a musician of their choice to assist them. Through their own observation and word of mouth, the family determines which musician can help with the healing. The relatives will approach the musician and say, 'We have this kind of problem in our family. We know you are effective with certain herbs. We believe you can be the one to help us.

Physic states: matter is energy vibrating at different vibrational rates. This is why when you go to a dance you find that you take on so many personalities in one night. You are not a schizophrenic. Each song has tuned into the matching vibrational rate within your body. When the match is made you find yourself rocking. It's like making love. When you and your mate like the same touch, stroke, caress, kiss there's no mountain you can't climb together — you vibrate on the same sexual frequency.

Awakening The Mother operates on much the same basis. You need music. You need her sound of power. Her Mantra. The first time I meditated to the mother's Mantra was at the Ausar Auset, society, a Pan African Religious organisation founded in the US. I sat in a community hall in West London with thirty-five other men and women from different professional, class and African cultural backgrounds. Our teacher Kemensi Napata, a highly skilled teacher and orator led us into our moment of peace. He switched on the music and with his gentle guidance we began to breathe in time with her words and music: Aung Vang Duhung Tua Auset En Aungkh,Nut, sai en hung. Thank You Mother Essence of Life.

As my inhalation and exhalation took me deeper into Self, I experienced a pleasant sensation of lightness. It felt as if no — things existed but the vastness of universe. Then the most beautiful thing happened — Spirit took me back to Trinidad the place I had spent a few years growing up and where I had lived out some of the most precious life moments. In my meditation I was a child splashing in the sea and running free on a white sanded beach. I was so happy. All through the meditation I felt light, breezy and very, very fresh. Afterwards, I had a wonderful feeling of being born again. I felt like the part of me that had been missing in my life had clicked right back into place. I told the whole room how I felt. I'm sure they thought I was crazy because I couldn't stop telling them: 'I feel born again.'

Meditating with the Goddess's words is a wonderful inner healing insperience. You feel nurtured, loved, revitalised as the feminine life force moves within you. becomes stimulated and begins to flow. In the power of her healing words you become a babe at her life giving breast.

THE MANTRA

A mantra operates on two levels (1) it quietens left side of your brain — the part of you that loves to chatter and be engaged in thoughts even at moments when silence is required. (2) It awakens the divine intelligent life force within.

Let's examine the first point. Close your eyes. Sit down in silence for a few minutes. Make an effort to stop the chatter in your mind. It's hard, isn't it. If you have started doing your meditations consistently you will find those thoughts become less intrusive with rhythmic breathing. The good news is — when you combine rhythmic breathing with the mental repetition of a mantra you will find it even easier to master the wayward mind. Not only will it have a rhythm to hook onto, but it will now also have words. Fortunately for us, but not so fortunate for Ms Chatter box the words do not have specific day to day meanings which can be analysed in the normal way. So Ms thang engages with them without the nuisance of her chatter.

Let's move onto the second point. As you know by now you are an internal as well as an external being. Together the two make the one. Ancient wisdom teaches us that our internal spiritual make up is made up of different energy levels which are the storehouses for the different aspects of our divine personalities. So within you there is the ability to intuit everything you need to know in your life. This part of your spiritual make up is known as your wisdom faculty, which is personified by the God of Wisdom Tehuti, Toth, Orunmila. There is another part of you which has the ability to choose. The choice is to follow the higher aspect of Self or the lower. This part of you is known as the Divine Will, personified by the God of Will Power — Heru, Shango, Jakuta. All in all it is said that we have about nine main spiritual personas. The aim of any spiritual system is to harmonise and balance us with all our personalities. When we are out of sync with any part of our inner life force, we are said to be out of balance with life and at dis-ease with Spirit.

Each part of your spiritual being has sacred words of power which vibrate at its frequency and stimulates it into action.

The mantra I am going to introduce you to in this chapter is known as The Auset mantra. It was brought back to us by my spiritual master and leader: Ra Un Nefer I, Divine King and High Priest of the Ausar Auset Society. It is available on tape. I recommend you get hold of it. The address is: The Ausar Auset Society, 197c Kilburn Park Road, London NW6 5LG.

MEDITATING WITH THE MOTHER

> *Let me be still and listen to the truth.*
> **A COURSE IN MIRACLES**

Before beginning the following meditation exercises, read through all the instructions carefully. If you want to enhance your meditation experience with your inner Goddess, you can look back to the chapter: Preparing Sacred Space, which will tell you how to set up an Auset shrine. Setting up this shrine will aid in the invocation and flow of your divine feminine energy.

EXERCISE: THE WORDS

Before even attempting your meditation you must first familiarise yourself with the Goddess sacred words. The words are to be chanted internally. Just a few words of encouragement. It may seem quite hard at first to remember them. Bear in mind learning anything new is hard at first, but with devotion, practice and effort you will get it.

Put a few hours of your day aside to memorise her words

> *Aung Vang Duhung, Tua Auset En Aungkh, Nut,*
> *Sah Aungkh en Aungkh.*

Aung Vang Duhang — are sacred words Power. They do not have a specific day to day meaning.

Tua Auset En Aungkh, Nut. — means thank you Auset, essence of light.

Sah En Aungkh — are The Mother's sacred words of power which stimulate the flow of the divine Life Force.

BREATHING
The words must be co-ordinated with Breath. For this part of the exercise, put aside a few hours in your day to practice harmonising the words and breathe.

> *Aung Vang Duhung, Tua Auset En Aungkh Nut*
> *Sah En Aungkh*

In. Out.   In. Out.

THE MEDITATION
There are two ways to meditate with the mother. You can breathe and mentally chant her words allowing her cool healing energy to bath you or you can choose

A Journey Through Breath

a limitation, or life problem you wish to tackle or change. I like to do the former in times when I am in need of The Mother's healing touch.

CONTEMPLATION MEDITATION
You will need thirty minutes for this exercise. It is recommended that you aim to do it once a day.
Close your eyes and take a few deep inhalations and exhalations.

Mentally chant the Mother's mantra.

After fifteen minutes you will find yourself in a deep state of trance indicated by the sensations you have already become familiar with from your previous meditations. The feeling of lightness or heaviness are the prime ones. From this point on you may get visualisations which come naturally into your sphere of awareness as the energy of the mother begins to move within. If you do receive any messages or visualisations. Do not hook onto them. Observe them passively as they float on by. Just continue to breathe, internally chant and enjoy the healing.

When you have come to the end of your meditation. Slowly open your eyes. sit quietly and write down your inner — speriences. Over a period of time, if you keep a consistent record, you will begin to notice common re-occurring messages, images and themes — all of which will give you tremendous spiritual insight into your universe.

Some of the most common visualisations you may have are:

Bathing, swimming, washing in water: A lake, river, sea, etc.

Being breast fed by a nurturing female. She is often a woman dressed in blue. Please note, if you do get this visualisation — there is nothing to be afraid of. It does not have any sexual connotations. If you look at pictures from ancient Egypt of Auset and child you will observe her feeding a child. Feeding indicates spiritual nurturing. So when you have this visualisation allow yourself to suckle at her breast freely. This is your time to be looked after. To have your needs taken cared of. To receive healing. Embrace it with an open heart.

You are a small child running, skipping, jumping etc. freely along a vast expanse of a sandy beach.

Being healed by a woman who may wash you with, water, oils, jasmine flowers etc.

Being a scarred small child who is comforted by a comforting female.

VISUALISATION MEDITATION

You will need thirty minutes for this exercise. It is recommended that you do it once every day.

Close your eyes and gently inhale and exhale.

When you feel sufficiently relaxed open your eyes.

On a piece of paper write down the thing you would like to heal most in your life. It can be anything from an illness to a bad relationship. (1) Write down the scenario exactly as it is at the moment. (2) Now write the scenario as you want it to be. So if your objective is to heal a bad relationship. You will first write down a typical frictional scene that keeps on happening between you and your partner. You may find you are always arguing over silly things or when it comes to intimacy your partner rejects you. Afterwards you will write down a scene which indicates the situation is healed. So with an argumentative relationship — you can visualise the two of you sitting down and talking through your disagreement in a peaceful loving way. Whatever it is you wish heal write it down as vividly as possible.

Once you have completed the above task. Close your eyes. Take a few deep inhalations and exhalations.

Silently chant the Auset mantra.

After fifteen minutes or on the moment you feel signs of trance — the main indicators being feelings of heaviness or lightness — start to work on your visualisations. Re-live the first scenario. Then follow it by the second. Make your visualisations real.

On completion of your meditation slowly open your eyes. Do not rush headlong back into your daily routine. Instead spend a few moments to re-focus and record your experiences in your spiritual journal.

SIGNS OF THE GODDESS

Mantras are extremely powerful. To know when your meditations have managed to invoke the particular energy you are working with, Universe provides certain internal and external signs called significators.

To know when your meditations with the mother are having their desired affect you need to know her internal and external signs.

INTERNAL
As The Great Mother is a nurturer, healer, and mother. You may find whatever illness you had such as a cold, or something more severe disappear. If your a hot tempered, impatient, anxious person you may notice you suddenly feel more relaxed, calm and peaceful. You may also feel much more nurturing and giving.

EXTERNAL
The mother has certain external associations connected with her energies. When she moves within you one or more of them may manifest in your life.

Her external associations include:

Day:	Monday
Number:	7
Colour:	Blue
Gems:	Pearls, Moonstone
Oil:	Jasmine, spearmint
Incense:	Jasmine, spearmint
Flora:	Lily of The Valley?

People and Career   Mother, Wife, Midwives, nurses, sailors, vagabonds, the masses, teachers of children, farmers, servants, menial employment, idlers, travel agents.

Foods: Water melon, lettuce, cucumber.

Miscellaneous: Pregnancy, romance, water, rivers, seas, visions, white items, women, tears

EXAMPLE

I work on many different deity energies throughout the course of my year. While writing this chapter it just so happened that I was doing internal work with The Mother. Two weeks into doing my contemplation's and meditations with her mantra, I received letter carrying some bad news from my bank manager, which threatened my financial stability. The news was received on a Monday — Auset's day — after I had done a beautiful meditation. The requested date in the letter for me to meet my bank manager to sort out the mess I had got myself into happened to also fall on a Monday. Needless to say on the day my bank manager was very nurturing, kind and supportive. The Mother was at work!

When I meditate with The Mother, I also find children tend to hang around me more. I spend more time in the bath pampering myself and I get a serious craving for watermelon!

Thursday 25th May

My meditation was very sweet and sad. At the moment I am crying and begging the forgiveness of my mother and father supreme.

This time I really focused on Breath and the meaning of mantra.

The visualisation that came to me was one of me being a small child. There were dark shadows all around me. I felt really scared and started to cry. This doesn't normally happen in my meditations. Auset held me tight as the shadows danced all around me. I was crying violently but she held me safe. In the shadows I saw my abuser, my school days and the time my cousin threw a book in my chest when I was younger — giving me a complex about my small breast. All the time I was seeing these things Auset held me tight. She then lead me in front of this huge waterfall. I wondered: 'what am I doing here' then I stepped underneath its cool waters and stayed there for a long time. I felt very sad and sweet all at the same time. I felt the need to forgive myself. I'm not sure for what, I just did.

Saturday 27th May

I have been feeling the need to release. I am not sure what, so I just meditated and contemplated the mother.

I saw snippets of my past again. At first I felt very heavy and weighed down. Then I began to feel lighter and lighter. I was a small child running in a flood of yellow light. At one point It seemed as if something bad was going to happen to me — before it could the Mother stopped it in its tracks. She then wrapped me in layers of purple silk and threads from the moon. The cloth and threads from the moon made a cocoon around me. Inside was very cool. I grew from an embryo to a child to an adult. When I reached adult hood the cocoon opened up and the moon light flooded in. Auset started to stroke and breast feed me. At this point I felt very sleepy, very serene. Towards the end of all of it I was sitting in a bright white light. All the time I was meditating with The Mother I felt a cool breeze blowing around my body and face. It felt very re-assuring.

I am Nature, the universal Mother, mistress of all the
elements,
primordial child of time, sovereign of all things spiritual
queen of the dead, queen also
of the immortals,
the single manifestation of all gods and goddesses that are.
My nod governs the shining heights of Heaven, the
wholesome sea-breezes,
the lamentable silences of the world below.
HYMN TO AUSET

Awakening the Goddess

THE GODDESS AND CHILD BIRTH

> *You are the bows from which your children as living*
> *arrows are sent forth.*
> KAHLIL GIBRAN

Last night I dreamt I had given birth to a baby boy. All I remember is meditating under a beautiful tree with huge fruits hanging down around me. Auset was perfuming my body and pregnant stomach with scented flowers. I remember The Mother talking to me, reassuring me and saying 'you are a spirit child giving birth to another spirit child. All will go well.' As she spoke and perfumed me I began to feel very calm and drowsy. I must have fallen asleep, because all I remember is in my meditation waking and being shocked. In my arms was a baby boy. It was weird. I had no sensation of giving birth at all. There was no pain as I slept.

Child birth is a natural sacred process and no chapter on The Goddess is ever complete without mentioning it. After all through her divine womb all things came into being. As through you your child comes to be.

When you give birth to the child growing within, you give birth not only to flesh and bone — but to an expansive intelligent life force. You give birth to Spirit. You give birth to a special gift from God. You give birth to an energy that has spent many lonely days and nights in the long queue for the return trip back to Mother Earth. When Spirit boards the celestial plane a magical journey of physical manifestation begins. In its dark, weightless world it transforms from no-thinness to cells, bones, skin, blood, organs. Every moment of its dynamic expansion is guided by the invisible hand of the Creator and you — the Earth Spirit, chosen to be its temporary gate-keeper.

Every emotion, mood, and feeling you have, while pregnant, is registered, absorbed, soaked up by your child's complex layers of sensory perception. Your child is an intelligent divine light tuning into everything you do — the way you eat, when you eat, what you eat. When you sleep, how you sleep. The way you think, reason, how you think and reason. Your biorhythm becomes her biorhythm. Your bio-chemicals become her bio-chemicals. When you are angry, she becomes angry too. When you are sad she becomes sad too. When you are happy she also is happy. In those early days and the days to follow you become your child's teacher. You teach her that the world is a fearful, angst ridden place. You teach her the universe is a place filled with love and possibilities. You teach her she is either wanted or unwanted. Your feelings will determine how she views her home-coming.

Toxic feelings will create a toxic baby. Trust me — I know. When I was pregnant with my son, I was very happy about the pregnancy, but at the same time I was wrapped up in an overwhelming amount of stress and anxiety. I worried about just everything. You name it and I worried about it — money, work, parenting. If someone had measured my worries against an angst monitor the needle would have gone crazy. I became so swallowed up in my own anxieties, I forgot one thing — to meditate. Oh yes, I meditated with The Mother sporadically but universe demands consistency. Something I wasn't and something I paid for, and boy didn't I pay for it. Instead of giving birth to serene peaceful young Spirit as hoped for, I gave birth to a screamer. My son could scream. I'm sure his crying could beat any opera singer's and shatter any glass. He screamed me and his father right out of our minds and house. for the first year of his earth bound existence he hollered, he bawled, for just about everything. He was clingy and wouldn't let me out of his sight. I was a nervous wreck. His father was a nervous wreck. Universe had taught us a lesson — you get back what you give out. I had gotten back all my worries tenfold. With all the worrying I had done during my pregnancy, it was no wonder why my poor son thought the world was a hostile place. I learnt the lesson and went right back to basics. I meditated and called on The Mother's assistance. I had to right my wrong. My child needed the reassurance he didn't get in his dark world. Needless to say things did calm down and I now have at the time of writing this chapter a very happy twenty month old boy.

In pregnancy you must carry yourself as you wish your child to be. you must become like a tree in Winter. Watch a tree in winter. What is it doing? It's standing there calm and serene against the harsh elements. It stands there erect and cool in a deep meditative silence, engaged in deep internal dynamic growth and expansion. The tree is at work. The work will pay off in its spring blossoms. In our modern day stresses and strains this seems like a tall command. For a large majority of us who face financial, relationship and life difficulties — an almost unrealistic one. Believe me it is not. Trust and consistent meditations with The Mother and her words of power will help you to create a balanced environment for you and your unborn child. It will definitely save on a lot of hair tearing once she/he makes an entrance!

The mantra can also be used to aid in the birthing process itself. Myself and many other women from The Ausar Auset society are proof of the eating. When I was pregnant with my son. I was determined to have a home birth and not to have any drug intervention. I was adamant my son was not taking his first glimpse into universe in a drugged out haze. I wanted him to see what he was coming into. I wanted him to have clear vision. Everyone, but my mother and partner and home-birthing midwives thought I was crazy. How on earth did I think I was going to have a baby at home and with no drug intervention? After all, it was my first child. That may have been the case, but I knew it was not my bodies first time. My body, like every other black woman's body is programmed with all the tools for safe child birthing. It holds the genetic memory of the safe natural birthing experiences of our mothers, grandmothers, great grandmothers and great great grandmothers

Before modern intervention, forceps, male doctors — women trusted in their own innate ability to give birth. We trusted in our own innate abilities full stop. We believed in ourselves. We felt empowered. We did not think in order to be happy we needed a man, lover, or husband to be a worth while person. We felt secure in the understanding that our first stop to happiness was ourselves. Of course, we believed in partnerships. We come from a people who believe in the power of togetherness, but we also understood Self love. Self love, means self-acceptance. Self acceptance means to be centred. To be centred is to be at peace. To be at peace is to operate from self-mastery. Birthing is an out flow of our internal power. When we can control how we give birth we exercise Self command.

For the last couple of months of my pregnancy I meditated with The Mother. Together we rehearsed Spirit through the birthing process. I visualised the safe passage of my son into the world. I visualised myself peacefully, and effortlessness giving birth. Often, while meditating visualisations of me standing in an ocean giving birth into its waters, would come and visit me. At those moments I knew — all would be well. I knew The Goddess within was at work.

By the time the day came Spirit was ready. Spirit knew just what to do. She had done it a million times before. Spirit performed beautifully. Spirit does not separate the unseen and the seen world. For her the two are one reality, in much the same way a the line between the sea and shore is not a line at all but the point at which they meet. Universe states: whatever happens on the level of the unseen has already happened on the level of the seen.

The contractions started. My partner rubbed my back. My mother quietly sat in a corner meditating. My midwives left the room. The Auset mantra played in the background. Together we visualised the safe passage of our little ancestor into his world. There was pain. I cannot lie and what a pain! There is none other like it. No dentist, surgeon, or boyfriend can inflict that kind of pain. The pain of child birth is the greatest pain you will most probably ever have to confront in your life. There is no getting away from that truth. Universe does nothing without a reason. It knows we need a little struggle before we get the blessing. Just think of the last time something came easy to you.

How does the saying go? There is no joy without... Yes, there was pain, but I felt very supported and in control. At no point did I cry for pain killers. I trusted in the power that flowed within me to help me do the work at hand. I meditated and called upon its strength to come and be my strength. I remembered all the women from our ancient and present lineage who had come before me and done the same thing with ease and grace. I remembered all our mother's who had stooped down on the earth of cotton plantations and trusted in their body's ability to re-remember how to give birth — when there was nothing else to turn to. In six and half hours, with no drug intervention, no doctor's interference or forceps. The Mother delivered my son fist first kicking and screaming safety into the world.

At this point it is important to emphasis that if you do choose to meditate with the Mother and her mantra during your pregnancy it must not replace your doctor or midwives care maintenance programme. The meditations are there to aid, and make your pregnancy an empowering joyful experience of grace and ease. To use the mantra to its full effectiveness I strongly recommend that you obtain a copy of it on tape from the Ausar Auset society.

EXERCISE: HAPPY CHILD MEDITATIONS
Perform this exercise for thirty minutes daily for maximum benefit.
Take a few deep inhalations and exhalations

Silently chant the mantra and combine your breathing in time with the words. Even if you are using the tape you must continue to silently chant the mantra.

Fifteen minutes into your meditation you will visualise yourself being peaceful throughout your pregnancy. Any situation in your life which is currently creating tension or stress, you will see yourself turning the situation around. Instead of your usual anxious, angry, etc. response you will see yourself acting with total peace, calm and serenity.

Write any messages, visualisations, insights you receive in your meditation down. Keep a note of your dreams, as well. It is a well known fact pregnant women seem to experience more than their fair share of prophetic dreams.

SMOOTH JOURNEY MEDITATIONS

Perform this meditation for thirty minutes daily for maximum benefit.

Take a few deep inhalations and exhalations

Mentally chant the mantra and combine your breathing in time with the words. Even if you are using the tape you must continue to mentally chant the mantra.

Fifteen minutes into your meditation you will visualise the mother helping you to give birth. you give birth with no effort or pain.

Write your insperience down in your journal.

Smooth Journey Meditation.

Write down all your insights, visualisations, dreams and messages.

Today I accept the universal Power of The Mother into my life whole heartedly and with joy.

7: THE ART OF LIVING JOYFULLY

> *All you need in the world is love and laughter.*
> *That's anybody ever needs. To have love in one hand*
> *and laughter in the other.*
> AUGUST WILSON

To all you travelling sisters reading this book: if you think you have to be serious, grave, austere, humourless, solemn, pensive, unsmiling and sad on the road to enlightenment, I've got news for you — Spirit says you don't. There's no divine law stipulating: 'The Journey must be travelled with a serious face and hard heart. There's no special plaque stating:î only those suffering from 'Delight Deficiency Syndrome' need travel hereî. In fact universe demands Joy. Joy for living. Joy for breathing. Joy for being just who you are, where you are, at the place you are.

Joy heals. Joy touches the spirit. Joy is the travelling shoes that empowers the will to carry out divine purpose. Without joy there is no laughter on the path, no love, no giving, no health of mind. Joylessness equates to disharmony — dis-ease with life. Where there is no joy there is no wholeness, there is no healing, there is no balance, there is no well being. Joy on the path will allow you to stay with the path. Joy in your heart will allow you to receive all the blessings and gifts universe has waiting to give.

Dr Lee S. Berk, a leader in immuno biology re-affirmed the power of joy through a series of experiments he conducted on five experimental subjects who viewed a 60 minute long humour video and five control subjects who did not. He discovered the simple truth — joy heals. In Eustress of Mirthful Laughter Modifies Killer Cell Activityî a paper published in Clinical Research he concluded: 'Mirthful laughter may attenuate some classical stress-related hormones and modify natural killer cell activity. Thus this eustress or positive emotion may be capable of immunomodulation. In other words, it is possible that, as Nietzsche so humorously postulated, îcontentment preserves one even from catching cold.'

A large body of work now supports his findings. In fact Western medicine is so impressed with the magnificent healing power of joy, centres dedicated to healing through happiness are rapidly spreading and recognition throughout Europe. Their philosophy is best summed up by the words of Dr Hunter D (Patch) Adams the founder of: Gesundheit Institute — the first humour hospital in Europe — 'The best therapy is being happy. All the other things the doctors can do are, at best, aids.'

If you are one of those die-hards who is still not convinced a little joy goes a long way, you better sharpen up your 'happiness skills' cause Spirit can't abide a miserable face, lack lustre, joyless approach to life. Divine law is quite clear on the matter: You can meditate, pray, fast, attend mass, give to charity, look after the old until the cows come home, if you can't turn up those lips, open up that mouth to laugh a bit and smile a little you ain't going no place on this spiritual journey very fast and as far as nirvana is concerned, you might as well forget about that.

BLISS BLOCKERS

It's easy enough to titter when de/stew is smokin' hot.

But it's mighty hard to giggle when/dey's nuffin in de pot.
PAUL LAURENCE DUNBAR

If I asked you to compile a list of the things keeping you from happiness right now, what would it look like? Compile a 'Happiness List' now. You can make the list as long as you want. An old list of mine read something like this:

I don't feel happy right now because:
I have no money.
I don't know where I'm going.
I haven't got a partner who loves and appreciates me.
I haven't got my career together.
My apartment needs decorating.
I have not got the wardrobe I would like.
I am too fat. When I lose some weight then I will feel happier.
I want more of a social life.
I feel drab.
I need some more intimacy.

Now make a 'Happiness List' of the things that are making you happy right now. Once again make the list as long as you want. My list read:

Right now I feel happy with:

1
2
3
4
5
6
7
8
9
10

Yes, you guessed it, I couldn't think of anything to put on my list. My guess is that you couldn't either. If you were floundering for things to list or listed things that were bringing you present joy and then dismissed most of them as less important than the future happiness you're chasing, you need to read on. You are in danger of missing out on life.

HAPPINESS IS…

Time is moving too fast, and I have too many things I
want to do. I think once you stop wanting to create,
wanting to work and push forward, you become old.
And Then you die.

DIANA ROSS

A very telling poll was conducted on 40,000 people. All were asked: 'what are your main goals in life?' Over 38,000 listed happiness or 'contentment as one of their main goals. The next question was 'Can you define happiness?' Only 1 percent of the pollsters could.

Spirit demands Joy. It craves it. It seeks it. It pushes us towards it. Yet still we seemed miffed on how and where to get it. Some of us interpret joy as achieving our goals. Others as getting recognition. Many as the magic formula found in love. Whatever the definition there is one thing guaranteed, it is often wrong.

As black women we have internalised at our own peril definitions of happiness based on outside approval instead of the power within. We have learnt from society that happiness is an 'outside in' thing, instead of an 'inside out' feeling. We have been told joy is the big house, posh car, handsome husband, first class university degree, smart kid, looks to kill for. We claim these mis-beliefs and travel our road. Breathlessly we run from point A to point B trying to attempt to acquire a piece of heaven. Like spiritual infants we chase the end of the rainbow looking for that pot of gold. In our mindless pursuit for more happiness we create our own sorrow. We fail to hear the gentle whisper of Spirit saying: 'You are Joy.'

Yinka needed to get the lesson but she refused to hear. She was one of those sisters who just couldn't sit down and enjoy the ride. She was so busy getting that she could not see she was busy missing out on the magic of life. I first met Yinka when I was invited to conduct a meditation workshop for a group of sisters who met on a regular once monthly basis. The group comprised of six busy career women, all dripping in money and to one degree or another highly strung.

Out of the six, it was Yinka who caught my eye. She seemed to be suffering from a particularly bad case of 'toxic success'.

At 25 most people would say Yinka had achieved. She had successfully completed her BSc Business & Management degree from London University graduating with first class honours. she worked for a well recognised financial institution in the city. In her out of office hours she ran a successful hairdressing business.

I was very impressed, like most, with her list of achievements and told her so. Unfortunately, Suffering from a severe case of 'twice as better', Yinka could not see why I was complimenting her on. As far as she was concerned she had much more to do and achieve with her life. She had much bigger goals to aspire to. She had an empire to build. As far as Yinka was concerned her life had not begun as yet and time was running out. She had to make it by the time she was thirty. It didn't matter that she could not define what 'made it' meant to me or anybody else, she just had to make it.

Those who only look on the surface of things would say Yinka was doing fine the way she was going. I like to look beneath the surface. What lay underneath looked less pleasant. Yinka was not well,

The Art of Living Joyfully

was not healthy, was not spiritually in shape. She suffered from a chronic case of asthma, stress, and tiredness. Her diet was out of sync with her bodily needs. She often grabbed her lunch and snacked on junk food. She did not exercise and she suffered from an overwhelming case of fear — not too uncommon for those of us busy trying to get somewhere. Under the glittering armour of her success Yinka was a spiritual mess.

After the meditation session, Yinka affirmed that she felt more relaxed, calmer, happier. She immediately concluded that she needed to do more silent contemplation and breathing exercises combined with a better more nutritional diet and aerobic exercise regime.

Then it began. The internal battle between God and Ego. The voice of God encouraged her in her new forward healthier thinking. Ego got busy defending its sanctified ground. As sometimes happens, the selfish voice of Ego drowned out the voice of God. Yinka began to change her mind. She liked the way she was feeling now. In fact she knew that a change in her diet, mind and spirit would help her stay on top of her asthma but she just didn't think she would be able to find the time. She had so much too do, she believed making time for herself would thwart her plans. I have not seen Yinka since that day, but I know Spirit will teach Yinka the only way she will listen — the hard way.

HAPPINESS IS…

Most of us define happiness from a spiritually immature belief system. We have learnt from society that happiness is the job, the car, the home, the villa in Spain, the baby, loads of money. Nobody has told us happiness is actually more than this and much deeper. We need to re-train our minds on what happiness really is.

Happiness is a way of being rather than another thing to do.

That's right. Happiness is not something you do or get. It is not another external acquisition. It is not even something that will necessary impress your friends. Happiness is that deep feeling of inner peace you have on a good day. It is the inside out contentment that mind, body and spirit crave. It is a feeling rather than a doing. A beingness rather than an action. It is eternal and constant. True happiness is forever unlike the temporal pleasures we seek to find it in. It is the original state of the heaven within. It was before things were. It is the everlasting love of the indwelling intelligence at work.

Happiness is…now

Happiness is not tomorrow when you achieve those far of goals. It is not some distant plan or dream. It is not some far off wild pursuit. It is not something you need wait for to happen. Happiness is now. It is right here and in this present moment. When you understand this you rid yourself of the frustration, the anger, the jealousy, the 'I didn't make it', 'I could of made it, 'I'm a failure' feelings. You Stop sacrificing your present happiness for some future better happiness. You relax into the universal moment. Allow yourself to live your life with more clarity, breath, vision and grace

'My happiness is now. My happiness is right now. Right here in this present moment'.

Repeat this to Self every day. Every morning on arising tell yourself: 'today is a good day'. Create a happiness diary. Put in it all the good feelings, things, emotions, people, jokes you come across during your day. Learn to take note of the small magical happenings in your life. It's time to re-train Spirit. It's time to stop wasting God's precious gift — life.

Happiness is a little...

Most of us are waiting for that time when we have more and bigger. Let's not fool ourselves: if you can't enjoy what you have now, it is unlikely you will be able to enjoy more. When you get the GTI, you want the Mercedes. When you get the Mercedes, you want the Porsche. When you get the Porsche, you want the Rolls Royce. Learning to enjoy what you have now does not mean you cannot aim to do or acquire better but it does mean that you learn to appreciate and work with what the universe has given you now. When you learn to say thank you to universe, universe feels better about giving you more. When you learn to use what universe has given to you in the present moment, universe feels confident in its decision to give. It knows you will wisely use what it has chosen to give you for the future.

If you were to die today, what are the things from your life you would miss. Stop taking what you have for granted.

Happiness is...connection

A study of 2,320 male survivors of heart attacks showed that more than cigarette smoking, high blood pressure, high cholesterol, diabetes and other well known health risk factors, loneliness was the primary cause of early death.

We do not stop where our bodies begins. We were not made as isolated individuals created separate from our fellow men and everything on earth. By our very nature we are a continuum of all that we see around us. We are part of the unending flow of universal energy which runs tenderly through the veins of all things. When we choose not to connect with our environment, Self and those around us we choose a life of separation, loneliness, un-wholeness. When we choose to lead separate, Self centred lives we break one of the most precious gifts — oneness. Reaching out, sharing and connecting with everything in the universe is the source of our internal well being. Th converse is to willingly invite the sickness of fear, feelings of lack of support, physical illness, and melancholy into our lives.

Today make an effort to connect in unity with someone or something. Take time out to connect with a friend, a lover or go to the park. Close your eyes and in-sperience the whole of nature. When you do this exercise make your connection from the heart and heart and not the mind. Make it a total experience.

Happiness is...a flow

Think back to the last time you did something effortlessly. When you seemed to be one with the task at hand. When you were so unaware of time that the hours just seemed to fly by. When you forgot about 'I', 'me', 'myself' and seemed to be part of something much bigger. When you were so joyous and totally focused on the moment. That was a time you were in the flow.

Flowing is a beingness. Flowing is an acceptance. Flowing is love. Flowing is patience. Flowing is joy. In flowing there is no resistance, there is no fear, there's no anxiety. In these precious moments we are at work hand in hand with the creative process of the universe. To flow is to open Spirit to receive the abundance of the universe. In the flow there is an acknowledgement and a becoming of. There's no doubt that flowing makes life so much easier.

Make today the day you commit to the flow. Notice the people, situations, events that happen and come to you during your day. Plan to have more days where you just flow.

Happiness is...having a good game even when you're losing

My flat mate loves football, I loath it, all the same by listening to him talk about his team and games I learnt an important lesson on happiness. Chi's team plays football twice weekly and without fail loses almost every match. The outcome became so predictable every time they went to play a match I knew he would come home and miserably state: We've lost again. I did what any good friend would do, I listened to his woes, gave him a pat on the back and like a lamb to slaughter he would go of again. If I got sick and tired of hearing about him losing, he was even more sick and tired. He was embarrassed, frustrated, and on the verge of giving up. Then one day after losing again and getting ready for the next lamb to slaughter repeat he turned to me and said: ìI'm going to make sure I have a good game, even if we lose.î They did lose again, but he had a damn good game.

Life can seem hard and unfair at the best of times. It can make us feel picked on. It can leave us with that 'why me?', 'why again' feeling. In simple words life can seem like a bitch. It can seem like the hardest thing to go on living. It can be the easiest thing to just give up on.

To find more joy in God's precious gift — life. You need to know how to laugh even when you feel you are losing. You need to know how to pick yourself up and go again. You need to get some valuable lessons. In life's hardship therein lies life's beauty. In the life adversities that come to visit your way, are the universal lessons that aid your spiritual growth. Without life challenges universe knows we remain spiritually immature — unenlightened. Without life's painful cross roads Universe knows that we keep on making the same old mistakes, in the same old way and get stuck in the same old groove. It is not universe's plan to punish you or inflict pain, sorrow, hurt and anger for the sake of it. The divine universal consciousness within wants you to grow and blossom, to be all that you can and more. Let's listen to the insightful worlds of the renowned philosopher and poet Kahlil Gibran: 'When you are joyous, look deep into your heart and you shall find it is only that which has given you sorrow that is giving you joy.'

Next time you experience a trauma, loss, pain, hurt, frustration in your life say to yourself: what is it that I need to learn from this lesson? In what direction is universe informing me I need to grow. It is also important to remember that no pain last forever. For every emotion experienced there is the opposite emotion waiting to be tasted. Where there is pain there is always joy waiting to be had.

Happiness is…exercise every day

Watch a baby learning, walking, talking, crawling, exploring for the first time. Notice how they do that particular activity over and over again until it is perfected. They don't care how many times they fall, stumble, graze their knees they will get up and do it again.

Changing our mis-learnt belief system about what brings us happiness and joy needs daily practice. You need to practice and practice: flowing, being in the moment, sharing, giving, picking yourself up when life knocks you down, connecting. Your desire for eternal happiness over your search for temporal pleasure needs daily chipping away at until it to becomes second nature.

From this day on commit to exercising your happiness muscle.

Happiness is...Enlightenment

Only those who are enlightened are truly happy. You know an enlightened person when you see one — they have a smile on their face, a bounce in their step no matter what. When you see them you may wonder, what do they have to smile about? They may not have the external trappings of success but what they do have is something much more precious and valuable — happiness. They are always smiling because they do not rely on transient things for their joy. External things come and go. They understand that those who rely on material things as their source of happiness are only happy as long as that thing last. They understand that external happiness does not last forever. When you are on a high you always have to come back down. The only thing that stays up is an enlightened way of being. Eternal happiness comes from an enlightened awareness. An enlightened awareness has no fear of losing things. An enlightened awareness is the spark that lights the flame of connection to centre, balance and the harmony that lies within.

From this day on commit yourself to travelling the enlightened way to happiness

The Art of Living Joyfully

Whatever you may have been told about happiness, joy and bliss, you need to stop right now and hear this. It may save your life: happiness is nothing more than what you have. Happiness is the majestic power you hold within.

No one can make you happy — not the boyfriend, child, cat or dog. No thing can make you happy. Acquisitions cannot make you happy. Winning cannot make you happy. Toxic success cannot make you happy. Happiness is not something you can go get. Happiness is simply a way of harmonious being. It is the inner way of feeling. It is the road of giving. The path of receiving. A journey of love. Happiness comes from such a deep blissful place, that it will heal you. It will heal you from your fibroids, your cancer, your misery, your depression, your anxiety, your jealousy, your fear. It will empower your vision, fuel your will, give you the balance and harmony needed to travel your road. True happiness is the eternal way of God.

He will hold up
The sky with life and support the
Earth with joy; his right hand
will support the sky with a
Staff and the left will support the
Earth with joy.
THE PYRAMID TEXT

To study Oshun is study the anatomy of joy.

To sit in quiet contemplation on her qualities and virtues is to come to a full understanding of the meaning of bliss.

When I think of this Erotic Goddess, I think of honey. I think of sweetness. I think of harmony. I think of love Oshun is the Goddess of Joy.

Her joy comes from a deep serenity of being one with everything and everyone around her. She is often depicted as a bringer of peace and social harmony.

She loves beautiful things.

In fact she is the original prima-donna.

Her beauty, grace and charm out shine all others.

Nothing can resist her joyful light. Her inner bliss acts as a magnet of powerful attraction.

Men, in particular find this stunning Goddess irresistible.

She is the juju Queen of Spiritual love.

She is the creative energy of God which heals depression, melancholy, and all female problems related to the womb.

She is the gift of vision and the energy, Ra, Kundalini, Life force which empowers the will to achieve our dreams.

Her motto:

My joy is my success. My success is a result of my joy.

One day all the Gods gathered in the Orun (The Realm of The Ancestors) to discuss a battle they were having with the Village of Women. They concluded that they would not win the war so under the instructions of Oba Orun, the Divine King of Heaven, they journeyed from their world to that of the Village of Women with a vow to end the war.

Sango (Spirit of Lightening), Ogun (Spirit of Iron), Omulu (Spirit of Infectious Disease) and Ibora Egun (Spirit of all those Warrior Ancestors who have passed) agreed to join hands in the battle against the Village of Women. They fought with great courage but met with bitter defeat.

Yemoja (Mother of Fish), Oya (Spirit of the Wind) and Iyaaami (Spiritual Mothers) agreed to join hands in the battle against the Village of Women. They fought with courage and conviction but met with bitter defeat.

When all of the Orisa and Egun from the Real of the Ancestors returned from their battle with the Village of Women they refused to engage in further combat. At that point, it was Orun (spirit of Joy) who said that she would put an end to the battle with the Village of Women. Osun placed a calabash of water on her head and danced from the Realm of the Ancestors to the World.

As Osun approached the Village of Women, she continued to dance and sing, using the calabash as a drum. When she had reached the centre of the village, the women joined with Osun. They danced and sang to the sound of her drum. The women of the village followed Osun to her shrine, where they dance and sing for her to this day.

YORUBA RELIGIOUS STORY

Today my world radiates with light and joy.

JOYFUL HEALING: LAUGHTER, MEDITATION

A little laughter, some tears — that's good, that's box office.
RICHARD PRYOR

I laughed so much until my belly hurt. I didn't realise sex could be so much fun. Mr PASSION INCORPORATE as I nicknamed him, was just what I needed after a quite sterile loveless life. He tickled me, he licked me, he found every ticklish point on my body. He found points I didn't even know about. While nimbling my waist, my shoulders, my elbows and ankles he cracked jokes, tickled me, made me laugh and experience several multiple orgasms — all at the same time. After five hours of love making and laughter with Mr 'P' I definitely felt healed.

Dr William Fry Jr Md, a leading mind/body scientist claims that 100 to 200 laughs a day is equivalent to ten minutes of rowing and jogging. When we laugh we make love to every internal organ in our body: our heart rate speeds up, breath quickens, circulation expands, oxygen intake and expenditure increases. In other words we are left with a very warm after glow similar to sex or exercising.

According to Dr Fry laughter takes place in two steps. Step one — the whole body is manipulated and stimulated. Step two — our relaxing neuro-hormones kick in making us feel relax and soothed after what is the equivalent of an exhilarating internal massage.

In fact laughter is such a powerful

mind/body/experience that it has been found to be a potent cure in deadly and life threatening diseases such as cancer. The explanation for this lies in the fact that laughter not only releases important healing hormones into our system, but it also helps us to look on the funny, humorous side of things. It is a wonderful tonic for dispelling the dark emotions of sadness, negativity, and depression. Laughter makes us feel good about who we are and life. It helps us to turn what appears to be a dire situation into something not so threatening after all. Ancient spiritual text tells us that laughter is a powerful cure for female sexual problems and a definite way to achieve enlightenment. When you laugh at your own folly or a life situation, what do you say don't you say: 'I feel lighter', 'I feel better', 'I feel more like myself again'. This is because laughter re-aligns you, it brings you back to your centre when you most crucially need it.

Laughter is celebration.
Laughter is kindness.
Laughter is love.
Laughter is acceptance.
Laughter is sharing.
Laughter is healing.
Laughter is forgiveness.

LAUGHTER AND BREATH
Laughter starts with a long drawn out exhalation. During the laughter stage the exhalations are longer

than the inhalations. During the recovery stage we are
often forced to take in and exhale long deep breaths.
We can happily conclude laughter is a form of
meditation.

EXERCISE
> Sit in a comfortable chair.
> Close your eyes.
> Take a few deep inhalations and exhalations
> Now laugh from the belly. Laugh like you
> really mean it.
> Do this for five minutes
> At first you may feel stupid laughing out aloud,
> but believe me you are really exercising your
> internal organs. If you really feel like a total fool,
> Just think of the great benefits you are getting.

INNER SMILE

When babies are not crying for food or because of wet
bottoms, what are they doing if not smiling? Once
they discover how to, they will do it all day long.
Smiling is a uniquely human experience. It is the first
language we speak as children. It is a powerful
transmitter of love, connection, and joy. Smiling lights
up worlds, dispels worry, anxiety, gloom. When we
smile we shrink our life problems by half. It is the
appreciative hug that says to the one you love thank
you for being all of who you are To share a smile with
someone is a gift of giving. To share a smile with Self,
is an internal kiss of radiant healing love. When we
give that inner smile to Self we post a brilliant light

force to our every organ, cell, muscle and nerve. Your heart beats one hundred thousand times every twenty four hours, without fail, until the day you die. Imagine giving a smile to your heart. Why not try it now? Imagine how it would feel. Why not try it now? Close your eyes and radiate a warm sincere smile to your heart. Uhmmm! Doesn't it feel good? Doesn't your heart feel lighter? Can you hear it smiling back at you with an appreciative hum? Imagine if you sent an appreciative smile to every organ in your body. How do you think you will feel? Wouldn't it feel good? Wouldn't it invoke the healing that you need, the balance you desire, the harmony you crave. Wouldn't you inhale and exhale easier into life?

From today on commit to sharing the warmth of your smile with a friend, stranger, relation, lover and don't forget Self. Nothing beats a black woman's smile!

INNER SMILE MEDITATION

The Inner Smile meditation is one that always goes down well with the participants of my workshop. It's deeply soothing touch is calm, relaxing and often much needed. It's a meditation I strongly recommend you incorporate into your daily meditation routine.

Put aside thirty minutes for this exercise

Sit in a comfortable chair

Close your eyes. Inhale and exhale deeply for a few minutes.

Starting from the crown of your head begin the muscle by muscle relaxation learnt in Chapter 4

You are now feeling deeply relaxed. Get ready to smile.

Begin the inner smile by smiling sincerely and lovingly into closed eyes. As you smile into your eyes Feel its radiant warm energy transmitting love and light. As it does so your eyes relax and smile right back.

Your smile begins its healing journey downwards. It flows into your jaw bone a place where so much tension is held. Your jaw bones acknowledge your smile you will feel your entire body relaxing, resonating and beginning to hum.

Your smile now radiates into your entire face. Every nerve, muscle, and cell becomes completely relaxed as it does so. Your whole face relaxes in the light of your loving smile. Pause and enjoy this special moment.

Flowing lovingly into your throat and neck your sensitive smile picks up on all the held in tension. Allow its warmth to melt away its hard edges. Feel its relaxing touch spread like a cool breeze to every cell, muscle and nerve in your body. It has a particularly tranquilising effect on the brain, to which the throat and neck said gateways to.

Your heart works so hard, give it an appreciative hug with your smile.

Recent research has discovered that the heart actually thinks and feels in much the same way the brain does. When we are upset, joyful or fearful, hormones are secreted from the heart as a physical response to these emotions. Our heart often knows

When we are having a feeling long before our higher brain registers it. Think of the things you say or feel in relation to the heart. When you are in fear or anger, don't you first feel a tightening, a constricting in this region, long before you can verbally formulate the thought you are afraid of? When you are in love, don't you just feel good and say 'my heart is overflowing with love', or 'I love that man with all my heart'? What about when you are in pain, doesn't it feel like your heart is breaking? In fact, isn't that what you say, 'I have a broken heart'.

As your smile radiates joy into your heart all the held tension is soothed, eased and released. Your body becomes completely and entirely relaxed as it vibrates love.

Enjoy this wonderful feeling for a moment.

Allow your inner smile to flow tenderly into your lungs. Feel your breath become easier, lighter and more centred as it does so. Smile deeply into your lungs moist environment. Allow them to inhale and exhale the light of your love. You are feeling even more relaxed, calm and content. Enjoy this feeling.

Your smile begins a slow gentle kiss to your assimilative and eliminative organs, without which you would be dead from toxic overload. Its journey begins with your liver, on the right side, just below your rib cage.

Direct your smile the two kidneys in, in your lower back, just below the rib cage on either side of your spine.

Let the healing dance of your smile to move into

your adrenals, they sit on top of the kidneys, your pancreas, your spleen and your digestive tract. Let your inner smile flow through all these vital de-toxing and assimilative organs until it reaches the navel. Let it rest there for a while as you radiate love to all your vital organs.

When you are ready let your smile go back to the place it began — your eyes. Allow it to smile lovingly into them once again. It's radiance travels down your spine and back to your navel. As it does so each of your twenty four vertebra, sacrum and coccyx are given a vibrant internal massage.

Your body is now vibrating with renewed energy and vitality. Relax and enjoy this invigorating feeling for a moment.

Daily Practice of the Inner Smile meditation will reap powerful benefits for your entire system and life. Not only will you internally oscillate at a calmer frequency, people will find you more approachable as you radiate love. If you find you are pushed for time and do not have the time to smile into each and every one of your organs. Simply close your eyes and allow your smile to radiate into your entire body. Start the smile from your eyes and let it flow all the way down to your feet.

Affirmation: From today I acknowledge the power of my inner smile. I promise to share its love with all those around me and to nurture Self in the warmth of its magnificence

The Art of Living Joyfully

VISUALISE WITH JOY

*In a consciously created image there must be the full
involvement both of thoughts, as well as, emotion. The
fresh image with fresh vitality imparted to it by emotion
has tremendous power against which the habitual image
cannot cross swords.*

ROHIT MEHTA

We all know about it, the die hard habit which can't or
won't be kicked. We've all been there, the booze, killer
cigarettes, addictive drugs, the appetite that seems to
have a life all of its own. We have all experienced the
frustration of trying to give these things up.

We all know old habits are hard to shake off. They
just keep on clinging and holding on. They will try
every trick in the book to keep their envied place.
Those old habits are selfish things. They don't care
that they are old tired news blocking you from
expansion. They don't care if they are blocking your
creative process. They don't even care if you don't
love them no more. All that that old worn out habit
cares about is staying alive and it sure knows how to
put up a good fight. It Knows how to make you feed
it, and keep it's limiting energy alive. When it's time
to get rid of that old habit, it's time to employ a little
touch of joy.

Joy is the energy of expansion. It is the upbeat
energy that makes you feel alive. When you
experience joy you feel light: you feel lighter. You

become more energised, more loving, more creative. Joy balances you. It makes you feel happy. It makes you want paint the town red, pink, blue, purple and gold. With joy in your life there is very little that can bring you down. A joyless journey is a journey of sickness. It is a journey which takes away Breath and brings death. When we apply the pleasure principle — whether it is calmer, more confident, peaceful, assertive, slimmer; we infuse it with an abundance of radiant energy. We strengthen it with the fire of universal breath and love, We make it strong. We win the battle.

Imaging is the means to change unwanted habit, but imaging without the intensity of emotion will get you no where. An empty cold image is no contest for the image fed by the constant repetition of old mind associations. It is definitely in a no win situation when you see that chocolate cake, you have been trying to give up for ages, and visualise with intense joy the pleasure the experience of its sweetness. To win the battle you must be able to create a vitalised image of walking joyfully past that lip smacking cake and eating your bowl of raw vegetables and salad with enthusiasm and bliss.

Visually rehearse the changes you want to make in your life with joy and pleasure and see your old tired behavioural habits wither away.

VISUALISING WITH JOY MEDITATION
You will need forty-five minutes for this exercise

Once you have prepared your room, close your eyes and take a few deep breaths.

Write down what it is you want to change or acquire in your life: you may feel shyness is limiting your success in life or desire a good loving supportive mate in your life. Write down (1) how the situation is now, in as much three dimensional detail as possible. (2) the new scenario. If you want to act less shy and with more confidence, create a scenario where, instead of acting in your usual shy manner, you act with confidence and Self assurance.

Close your eyes again and start your deep abdominal breathing When you feel the signs of trance relive the old habit scenario you wish to change, for 15 minutes. Followed by a further fifteen minutes of visualising the new desired mode of behaviour you wish to adopt. You must live out the latter with joy. So if you are trying to give up cigarettes, see yourself joyfully enjoying a fitter healthier lifestyle without cigarettes.

When you have finished, use your twilight time to write down in your spiritual journal any thoughts, insights, messages, difficulties, you may have experienced in your meditation.

TIP BOX
Make your image as real, vivid and three

dimensional as possible.

Visualise it as if it is happening now and not in the future. The brain only recognises what is in the present not the future. If it is convinced an image is something happening now it will along with the nervous system treat it as an actuality and act upon its physical manifestation almost immediately.

Infuse your image with as much joy as possible. The brain does not respond to compulsion, or pain, only pleasure.

Make your image positive. So if you want to be healthier see yourself joyfully living the life of a healthy person.

Visualise your image often.

STATEMENTS FOR JOYFUL LIVING

Remember that the antidote for hubris, to overweening pride is irony, that capacity to discover and systematise ideas. Or as Emerson insisted, the development of consciousness consciousness consciousness. And with consciousness, a more refined conscientiousness and most of all, that tolerance which takes the form of humour.
RALPH ELLISON

I am joyful therefore I am successful.
HET HERU

The Art of Living Joyfully

There is hope for the future because God has a sense of humour and we are funny to God.
BILL COSBY

If you eat sweet things and avoid the bitter kola, all food will loose its flavour.
IFA PROVERB

If you don't have a sense of humour, you become a scowling time bomb. Striking out at people who are dear to you.
ISMAEL REED

They seem to me like the gayest and bravest people possible — these Negroes from the Southern ghetto-facing tremendous odds, working and laughing and trying to get somewhere in the world.
LANGSTON HUGHES

Those who do not know suffering cannot experience pleasure.
IFA PROVERB

Being on the road gets rough sometimes, but I'd sure miss singing to the people. **ELLA FITZGERALD**

No matter how difficult things are, we can laugh.
DENG MING-DAO

*There is no achievement of the will without energy, and
no extraordinary achievement of the will without an
intensification of the power of the nervous system,*

or without intense emotional pleasure.
RA UN NEFER AMEN

*The body becomes a realm of joy, because no external
circumstance can disturb that person's presence of mind.*
DALAI LAMA

*Only the enlightened are consistently happy, because their
happiness is not predicted upon the events and
experiences that take place in this world. Instead it is
based on the boundless inner energy they gain from their
connection with the world of enlightenment.*
DR FREDRICK LENZ

Light and joy and peace abide in me.
A COURSE IN MIRACLES

I found out life's hard but it ain't impossible.
AUGUST WILSON

The Art of Living Joyfully

The blows rain. The men sing.
ERIC WALROND

---

*Once you've danced, you always dance. You can't deny
the gifts that God sends your way.*
JUDITH JAMISON

---

*Life — an infinite loving
Sweeping to the peak of anticipation
Trembling breathlessly at the brink
Of realization.*
FRANK HORNE

---

*I wish to live because life has within it that which is good,
that which is beautiful, and that which is love.*
LORRAINE HANSBERRY

This is just life; it's not to be cried over, just understood.
RALPH ELLISON

Life is short and its up to you to make it sweet.
THE DELANEY SISTERS

---

*I find in being black, a thing of beauty: joy, a strength, a
cup of gladness.*
OSSIE DAVIES

> *My future starts when I wake up every morning.*
> **MILES DAVIS**

> *Believe in life.*
> **W.E.B DU BOIS**

> *This is the urgency: Live!*
> *And have your blooming in the noise of the whirlwind.*
> **GWENDOLYN BROOKS**

> *I'm on my own feet. Learning to stand, to walk, to dance.*
> **JOHN EDGAR WIDEMAN**

> *Haste has no blessing.*
> **SWAHILI PROVERB**

> *I believe in the Power that dwells within*
> *to provide all my needs.*
> **AFFIRMATION**

I plunged into the job of creating something from nothing.
Though I hadn't a penny left, I considered cash money as

The Art of Living Joyfully

*the smallest resource. I had faith in a living God, faith in
myself, and a desire to serve.*
MARY MCCLEOD BETHUNE

---

*Your power is in your faith. Keep it
and pass it on to the bloods.*
MOLEFI KETE ASANTE

---

*Anybody who has kept up with my career knows that I've
had my share of problems and trouble, but look at me
today. the years, no matter how much success I
achieved, I never lost my faith in God.*
ARETHA FRANKLIN

---

*Quit talking about dying; if you believe our God is all-
powerful, believe He is powerful enough to open these
prison doors. Pray to live and believe you
are going to get out.*
IDA B. WELLS

Accept finite disappointment, but never lose infinite hope.
MARTIN LUTHER KING, JNR

Keep hope alive, keep hope alive, keep hope alive.
JESSE JACKSON

225

The rhythm persisted, the unfaltering common meter of blues, but the blueness itself, the sorrow, the despair, gave way to hope.
RUDOLPH FISHER

Love stretches your heart and makes you big inside.
MARGARET WALKER

I believe that unarmed truth and unconditional love will have the final word and reality. This is why right temporarily defeated is stronger than evil triumphant.
MARTIN LUTHER KING, JNR

In the infinite reality of life there is an overflow of love which eases my hardest day and fills my life with joy.
AFFIRMATION

Because I had loved so deeply
Because I had loved so long
God in His great compassion
Gave me the Gift of song.
PAUL LAURENCE DUNBAR

8: LIFE

After I was initiated. I initiated myself.
IFA PROVERB

Take a few deep breaths. You are now ready to open your eyes. Welcome back, you have journeyed far. In your travelling. In spirits silence you found pain, yes there was pain. You found resistance, yes there was resistance. You found hurt, yes there was hurt. You found anger, yes there was anger. You found confusion, yes there was confusion. You found sadness, yes there was sadness. You found rejection, yes there was rejection. You found tears, yes there were tears. Then you found healing. You found balance. You found a deeper connection to Spirit.

Through claiming your pain. Through ownership of your hurts. Through the embrace of responsibility. Through the control of breath you discovered your silent pool. Your centre of magnificent. Your depth of clarity. Your inner strength. You found POWER. You found the kind of power you thought someone else possessed, but not you. You found the kind of power: the power of inner stillness, of inner knowing, of inner grace, of inner transformation, that has made you realise you are more than what you had been told, you are more than what you feel, you are more than the reality of your own rational mind. Through connecting, you discovered a new way of being, a new way of doing things. You discovered

CREATIVITY. The power, the ability, the love in action which makes you the master of your own destiny.

Through your spirit's silent journeying you took a leap forward into mastery. The test now is — life. Meditation does not stop with the opening of the eyes. It does not stop when you go through your door. It does not stop when the lights go on. It does not stop when you blow out the candle. It does not stop when you get up to go to work. True meditation begins with life. When you can keep your breath through the accusations. When you can keep your breath through the pain. When you can keep your breath through the hurt. When you can keep your breath when the bill arrives or when the car is taken away. When you can keep your balance in adversity. When you can keep your peace, your Amen, your hetep, your centre in the midst of some of life's most adverse situations, you have begun the true meditation. To inhale and exhale, deeply and rhythmically through all life has to offer — the good and the bad — is the key to spiritual success.

'But', I can hear you say 'I was told that meditation will make my life more peaceful, more serene, more balanced.' Yes it does. Meditation does change your life. It does give you all these things, but not in quite the same way you have been led to believe. The mere act of happens when you taking quiet time with Self will, with consistent practice, make you more serene. But the test comes when you step into life. Your problems have not gone away. They have not suddenly disappeared in a puff of pink smoke. They have not been taken away by some magic genie. As soon as you open your eyes it's all still there and sometimes even more.

Think of a holiday. When you go for your break away to the Caribbean, To Africa, To Europe. How do you feel? Don't you feel more relaxed, more peaceful, more clear headed? Don't you suddenly feel as though you have the space to approach life in a different more creative way? Don't you feel like your batteries have been re-charged? Don't you feel you will now be able to handle the bills, the bad relationship, the boss who gives you grief, the job you hate? Don't you feel good? Don't you feel lighter? Don't you feel renewed? Meditation is like taking a holiday. It recharges your battery for the confrontation of life's challenges. It clears the mind, strengthens Spirit, expands consciousness. It gives you right thought and allows for right action. Meditation is the training ground for life.

It is easy to be comfortable and altruistic when we are sitting comfortably in our seats, but the test of the practice is when we encounter a problem.

DALAI LAMA

Living is the stage of meditation which catches most would be meditators out. The books do not prepare the interested traveller for this crucial part of the spiritual journey. If you cannot put to practice what you have learnt during meditation and apply it to life, all purpose is lost. You have missed the reason behind the golden breath. You have travelled all this way only to miss out on the pot of gold. Meditation is a spiritual gem. It is a tool. Like all tools it has a function. You do not buy a car without knowing how to drive it — what is the point of that? You do not have a spade and not know what to use it for. You do not buy a camera and neglect to learn how to operate it. You do not acquire things without knowing their purpose. Purpose is the reason for why a thing exist. Purpose is the motivating force that carries us forward. Without purpose there is no point to living. Without purpose all essence is lost. Purpose is the why behind the I. When you understand meditation is the internal gift of external power, you understand its purpose. You have understood its function. You can utilise it to the wholeness of its essence. You can continue your journey without giving up. Without feeling cheated. Without feeling your cultivated silence has been a waste. You can by pass the trap that makes most meditators stumble and fall.

I had a Buddhist friend, who loved Buddhism, but hated to meditate. Her complaint, every time she meditated something bad happened to her. She was more irritable, more aggressive, she even seemed to have more debt. In the end she gave up both meditation and Buddhism. She gave up on the very gifts that gave her clarity and the balance for living. She gave up on herself and Spirit. Universe has seen many casualties on the path. Casualties who have travelled half the way only to give up on the other half — the most important half.

To be a successful meditator you have to understand the bag of tricks ego will lay your way in life. You have to understand how to safe guard your spiritual growth. You have to know the rules of the game. Knowing is awareness. Awareness is not a magic cure for life's dilemmas. It does not take away the edge out of living. It does not take away the pain and the hurt. It does not take away the lessons. To take away the lessons is to take away life itself. Awareness is the guiding light which will help you to walk your path with courage and a smile. It is a guiding gem, a gate keeper for those difficult moments. Awareness let's you know that when you fall you can pick yourself up, dust yourself off, and try again — that's what life is about.

> I open my eyes to
> the universal flow of
> life.
> I open my eyes and there is balance.
> There is seeing.
> There is peace
> because I am one with God.
> One with my inner energy.
> One with Breath.
> One with the universal life force.
> One with me.

MEDITATION TRAPS
There are many things to make you fall, make you

stumble, make you want to give up the meditation journey. These are the things you need to be aware of.

THE CHALLENGE

Elegba, the Yoruba God of the cross roads loves to bring life challenges to us. His work is even more rewarding when we are at total peace. Peace is his playground. He will look deep into the reflective pool of your soul to discover the one thing that will ripple its coolness. Then he will play with you, tease you, cajole you, all in a bid to heal you.

Whatever you are meditating on is the very challenge that will come to visit you. If you are meditating on peace, you will encounter challenging situations which will attempt to disturb it. If you are meditating on overcoming low Self esteem, you will be faced with situations were you have to assert yourself. If you are meditating on anger, you will be put into life situations which will provoke you to anger. If you are meditating on jealousy, a beautiful woman will cross your path.

Your meditations will take you to a higher place and bring you to a valley. The valley is the places, spaces and moments in your life where you have that same old feeling — again: the anger, the shyness, the low Self esteem, the hurt, the pain, the sadness — all come back to revisit. The valley is the opportunity given to you by universe to invoke Spirit over matter. Valleys are beautiful places to be. They are the luscious processing rooms for purifying Spirit and putting its new programme to work. The valley offers you the opportunity you have been waiting for — growth.

When you are confronted with a valley. A cross road. A life dilemma keep your breath. Take a step back. Remind Self that in your silent sitting you have given power to Spirit. You have connected Spirit to a higher consciousness, a deeper wisdom, a broader understanding. In every life challenge you now have the will to assert the mastery of Spirit over ego. Quietly affirm to Self: 'In every valley. At every cross road. In every life dilemma I remain at peace. I remain in control through the power of the divine breath.'

DOUBT

There are many times on the path when you will doubt. You will doubt the purpose for meditating. You will doubt your desire for spiritual growth. You will doubt, doubt, doubt. Doubt will make you want to give up. It will make you feel like you are wasting your time. It will make you question if what you are feeling and insperiencing is real. Doubt is tricky. He knows many ways to ease you off the path. He has rehearsed a hundred thousand times with a hundred thousand casualties. Doubt is the gentle whisper that tells you: 'give up'. It is that insistent nagging voice that plays on your fears, your weakness, your scepticism.

I have doubted my journey many times. I have given up travelling on many occasions. I have questioned the purpose of my meditations more times than I can remember. When you come to those down

233

moments, its time to analyse. Doubt must be put under the spotlight of analysis. There will be times you will find your doubts to be real. When put under close examination, doubt will often be found to be the fearful life call of ego holding on for breath. When this is the case you must discard with it and summon the strength to move on.

Affirmation 'When I doubt. I analysis. When ego makes me want to give up I draw upon the Breath of life and I move on.'

FEAR

My fear played havoc with me. It did not like the idea of the sweat lodge. Crawling on all fours through a small hole, sitting on the mother earth with no clothes on, in complete darkness and intense unbearable heat was not its idea of fun. The closer the time came the more my fear rose. The more my hands dripped with sweat. The more my head began to throb. Fear knew it was too late to look back, but it still worked hard to hold on.

There are many moments during meditation when you will feel fear. You will fear you are going crazy, will get lost in a dark unknown void, a force will take possession of you, friends will be lost. Your fears will be many. They will make you want to give up. If you give in to fear it will make you miss out on the magic.

When you are faced with fear, like doubt, put it under examination. Under close analysis you will find that fear is often nothing but fear of the

unknown. In this culture we have been taught to fear
the unknown. To attach a negative meaning to it. Fear
is not negative. Fear is positive. Fear tells us we are
about to take our first step into power.

Affirmation 'I face my fear with courage. I face
my fear with the knowledge that I have a beautiful
journey to travel. I commit to the process and my fear
dissolves.'

DISTRACTIONS

There are many times you will feel bored with the
practice of silent sitting. There will be intervals when
the spiritual path seems down right dull. In these
moments you may want to go back to the old way of
doing things. Ego's way of doing things. You may
want to whoop it up on a momentary high. You may
do things to make life feel more exciting. You may go
and pick that argument, cuss out the boss, rile up your
boyfriend, bitch at someone you love. For that instant
you may feel a sense of exhilaration, a sense of release,
a sense of gratification. But something deep inside
you will still crave eternal peace over the temporary
high of ego. Your awakened higher Self will gently
call you back to centre. You may go back willingly.
Often we go return with reluctance. Returning back to
the path in reluctance has its danger. It will leave you
vulnerable to ego's next boredom call.

Boredom on the path can only be dissolved
through understanding. Understanding gives us a
knowing. Knowing is the wisdom of right perception.
Right perception informs us that boredom is ego's

addiction to a momentary high. When we are high we feel good, alive and joyous. However, the high does not last for long. After every high there is a low. These low periods last longer than the high experienced — meaning 80% of your life experience is spent at a low with only peaks of bliss. What a way to live!

Wisdom informs us: why have a temporary taste of freedom when you can have it all? It helps our minds to understand there is such a thing to life as continual bliss. It re-tunes it to the more steady, more balanced, more serene energy flow of on going happiness. It teaches it continual bliss is the high that never brings you down.

Let ego go. Release its need for the transient moment. Free up your universe to eternal peace.

Affirmation 'I embrace the flow of my universal moment'

DISORIENTATION

After my first meditation I remember clinging onto my partner's arm for the whole day. I was terrified I was losing it. I felt as though I was having a nervous break down. Nothing on the outside world appeared to be the same. Familiar things suddenly looked strange and different. The people, the buildings, events didn't seem to be as I remembered.

No one had warned me that the early stages of meditation often brought about moments of disorientation. Disorientation is nothing more than the old way of perceiving things breaking down. Meditation Purifies the mind. It connects it to a higher state of universal consciousness. It takes the traveller beyond the secure mental prison of worn out perceptions. It liberates us into growth.

As a first time meditator you will find there will be moments of disorientation on your path. Like myself, you may feel like you are going mad, losing it, losing a grip on reality as your mind expands beyond the boundaries of your set mental notions. If unprepared for this experience you may very well give up, never to return to the meditative path again.

The anti-dote to disorientation is non resistance. Non resistance will allow you to accept the new and let go of the old without fear. It will aid in your spiritual transformation. Exercising Patience and Acceptance will help aid Spirit in new adjustments.

In moments of disorientation on your journey. Breath and know you are safe. Breath and know nothing is going to hurt you. Breath and know you are not going to go mad, you are not going to lose it, you are expanding into a new higher form of consciousness. New growth always feels strange at first. Don't fight the changes you feel occurring. Do not retreat back to your old self. Have courage and patience — allow for Spirit's growth. Relax into the moment and repeat the affirmation: 'All is well in my world.'

HIGHER ENERGY

Meditation brings with it a new lease of life. A new burst of energy. This energy is the fuel for Spirit to carry out divine purpose. It is the fuel which will take you to a higher place. The problem lies in life.

Once you open your eyes and greet the outside world, your old habits are still there. It is a process of time and consistent practice before their grip is loosened. In the mean time there is the temptation to use your new found energy in the service of Spirit. You may find your sexual potency, attraction, charisma, enthusiasm are enhanced. When this is the case it is wise to remember these are the side benefits of meditation and not its goal. The end purpose of meditation is to gain a higher wisdom and balance in your life. Along your journey you may find you are in need of higher Self esteem. It's okay to meditate on increasing it, as long as you keep in mind your objective for desiring more — to live a healthier life — not to gain points over other people.

When you are tempted to use your new found power, charisma, confidence, in the wrong way take a few deep breaths and repeat the affirmation: 'With each and every day. With each and every breath I commit to a higher wisdom. I commit to a higher knowing. I commit to the growth of my eternal light.'

COMPARISON

When I meditate I have the most fantastic visualisations visit me. Spirit and the ancestors talk to me through image. I have vision, you may feel, smell or hear things. You may not have any of these insperiences and just feel a deep sense of inner peace.

Life

SPIRITUAL PRIDE

Without humility and compassion on the path you are in danger of falling prey to one of ego's nastier traps — spiritual pride. Spiritual pride empowers ego and leaves God consciousness stranded. It will slow you down and way lay you on the road. The person puffed up with spiritual pride is under the sad illusion they are better than every body else. They are judgmental, over-critical, and arrogant. Simply put they have missed the point.

When ever you feel you are in danger of catching a dose of spiritual pride affirm to Self that meditating, praying, libation pouring, does not make you more spiritual than any one else. It does not make you better. It does not make you holier. It does not give you the right to invalidate other people's experiences. Practising humility will help you to understand that you, like the other person, are a traveller on the long road to enlightenment. Practising compassion will help you to embrace each persons journey as unique.

BALANCE

I am because we are; and since we are, therefore I am.
JOHN MBUTI

The bliss of the meditation experience is an experience beyond this world. It is beautiful and shines with light. While writing this chapter I conducted a meditation workshop with first time

239

meditators. The workshop was part of a female healing retreat in London. The session was held just before breakfast. The idea was to refresh the retreat participants for the rest of their day's process. It so happened that once the meditation was finished no one wanted to go for breakfast.

The silent moment is truly enchanting. Like everything that enchants there is a danger you don't want it to go away. You want it to stay. You want to stay with it. I know many people, people who are close to me, who spend hours upon hours just meditating. In the meantime, their relationships, marriages, finances, and life fall apart. Meditation is not an excuse to neglect your family, your relationships, your life affairs. It is not an excuse to cop out of life. Meditation is about inside out balance. The secret of the successful meditator is to be in the world but not off it.

At every moment of your meditation journey look around you and see what you are neglecting. What are you running from? What are you are not confronting? Those are the situations you need to right. Do not neglect your family, lover, husband, child. You are part of a connected whole. You are part of society, part of the world. Share what you are learning with others. Give love and take responsibility for your life events. Listen to the wise words of the Dalai Lama when he says, 'I usually advise people to devote half their time to the affairs of the world and half their time to the practice of the teachings. This is a balanced approach for most people.'

Study

In your waking meditation state you must study, study, study. I cannot emphasis enough how important it is to study on your journey. Go into the bookshops, buy as many books as you can on meditation, spirituality, African wisdom traditions and study them, enjoy them, trust your intuition and take from them what is necessary for your travels.

Without study on the path — it will be like driving a car with no hands — you are bound to crash. Study will help broaden your spiritual perspective, tune you in to alternative ways of thinking, give you knowledge of other's journeys. Study will make you realise you are not alone on the path. You are not the only one going through what you are going through. You are not the only one finding your way.

Studying will inspire, motivate and help you in your dynamic transition from darkness to light. It will give you the informed awareness to stoke the fire of enthusiasm, the fire of persistency, the fire of love. It will aid in the awakening of your mind and cultivation of your spirit. It will strengthen you against ego's bag of dirty tricks.

If I had not studied on my path I would not be where I am today, I would not have met the people I have met, or had the love, understanding and enthusiasm I have for spirit today. In fact if I hadn't studied I would have most probably concluded that what I was feeling, what I was desiring, the path I had chosen to travel was all very weird and strange. I would most probably have given up. Studying tuned me into the knowledge that I was far from weird. I was one of many spirits re-finding the way home.

Do not limit what you study. Read as much, and as widely as you can. Read books from your own as well as different ancient cultures. Remember, on the path you are a student of life.

FINDING A TEACHER

> *When the student is ready, the teacher will come*
>
> PROVERB

My first teacher came two days after I had a dream about a train journey.

In my dream I was on a train destined for Africa. I was also in a big dilemma — did I want to get off at the final stop or not? My dilemma increased as I thought about the prospect of having to leave my family and long standing acquaintances in London behind. The journey was long. The train chugged on. I had enough time to fret and chew over things. I had enough time to decide on my destiny — I eventually committed — I was getting off.

I have never forgotten the vividness of the colours of the scene which greeted me. Africa greeted my feet with the first touch of soft white virgin sand. Her aqua green sea blessed my feet in her salty waters

I was ready for my journey. I had no idea of where I was going. I embraced trust and walked with her. I had covered a short distance before coming across a group of playing children. We did not speak the same language yet somehow they instinctively seemed to know where I had come from and where I should be going. Led by their reassuring hands I found myself standing alone at the top of a white sandy hill overlooking a group of laughing chatting women. I was immediately struck by the fact they were all wearing black as if in mourning and their stunning midnight beauty.

I stood on top of the hill for quite some time until something — maybe my thoughts, maybe my feelings, maybe my need to be part of their ancient energy stream — made one of the women in the group turn around to look at me. The rest followed her gaze. I recognised them, they recognised me. We seemed to have met a long time ago on these same shores. We re-connected through tears, grief, joy. Their open arms embraced me as one of their own. Spirit had been welcomed home.

On awakening from my deep sleep I automatically knew I had to change my name. I knew the dream had something to do with the new name I would later carry, but I wasn't sure what the connection was. Two days later in my college library I met a small in conspicuous looking man from West Africa. I had never seen or spoken to him before, but my spirit felt drawn to speak to him. He turned out to be Oggonna, an Igbo high priest doing his PhD in

London. We spoke for hours, He interpreted my dream and gave me my name — Ezolaagbo — one who returns home. Oggonna became my first spiritual teacher in the long line of the many to come. He awakened and enlightened my spirit.

Teachers come in all shapes, ways and forms. They often come when we are ready to walk with guidance. They are sent to us by universe. When your teacher comes you will instinctively know is your teacher. Your teacher is someone you will feel an immediate connection with. He or she will be someone you will feel a great love and respect for and they in turn will feel the same love and respect for you.

The teacher you meet now will not necessarily be the teacher you will have tomorrow. Your teacher from yesterday may not be the right teacher for your today. Teachers come at the right time, with the right knowledge, at the right place. The teacher you meet now will have the right qualifications and knowledge you need for your spiritual journey at this particular moment in time. He or she may have a small or large thing to show you. Whatever the size of the gift it is the very tool you are in need of at this point of your journey to keep you growing.

At the beginning of your meditation journey it is important to seek a teacher. Of course you can start off by exploring meditation at home, but it will soon become evident to you why you need a meditation teacher to guide you on your path.

Find a teacher by making enquiries at your local

yoga and health centres, flick through the national and local health publications, ask friends to recommend someone. When you have eventually decided where is it you want to go, go with an open mind and heart. You will soon know whether the teacher you have found is the right one for you. Indeed you will soon discover if they are a good teacher. 'How do I know when I have found the right teacher?' you may be asking. Simply put, a good meditation teacher is someone who help you attain the meditation state. This might sound like a ludicrous reply. Be warned, there are many people who go to meditation classes who have never experienced not even the slightest glimpse of the aware mind.

A recent case in point is a friend of mine. While writing this chapter she called me a few minutes past midnight. She informed me that she had been going to a meditation group for a few months. She was concerned. Something was not quite right about her teacher but she could not put her finger on what it was. During our hour long conversation it transpired in all the time she had been going to his group she had never experienced the state of the meditation trance. Her intellect concluded that she just wasn't the 'right type' of person for meditating. Spirit knew something was wrong with the teacher.

I asked my friend if her teacher had taught her and the class the basic keys to meditation such as Breath. She confirmed my suspicion — he had not. In fact not only had he not taught them the basics, he informed them they were not ready to learn the basic rules! That was the most ludicrous thing I had ever heard. I told my friend so. She now has another teacher.

Your meditation teacher should be qualified. He or she should know the basic rules of how to help someone achieve the meditation state. If they do not your spiritual progress will be put back ten steps. A bad teacher can way lay your journey.

Whoever you choose as your teacher should be a vessel over flowing with abundant warmth and compassion. He or she should be able to identify with your life experiences and help you to transform them into beautiful lessons. As a teacher he or she should be practising what they preach. They should through the meditative path be diligently striving to tame their own mind. If not, how can they help you to?

You should feel comfortable with your teacher. However, I have one little word of warning: when uncomfortable and critical of your spiritual meditation teacher, first examine your own mind. Put your feelings under analysis. If it is ego resisting change analysis will soon highlight this.

Change is often a difficult thing. Old belief systems are hard to let go off. They will fight for their right to live. When they are challenged, they become enraged. They become irritable. They direct that irritability at the person threatening their existence. That person may be your spiritual teacher. Spiritual law teaches us: criticism is often fear masked. When you are feeling critical of your teacher or someone close to you, ask your self what it is that you fear letting go off.

THE SEVEN SPIRITUAL LAWS OF SUCCESS

UNCONDITIONAL LOVE
GOOD DEEDS AND WORDS
POSITIVE THINKING
LETTING GO
SELFLESSNESS
ASKING
GRATITUDE

The seven spiritual laws of success will help to further aid you in your spiritual growth. Practice them in conjunction with your sitting meditations and make each day of your life worth while and harmonious.

UNCONDITIONAL LOVE

> *Love is giving, seeking nothing in return.*
> **EGYPTIAN PROVERB**

When you give don't you expect something back in return? Isn't that what it is all about — giving to receive? How can you give without getting? Isn't getting part of the deal? Since childhood getting is what we have learnt giving is all about. We have internalised the notion without getting there is no point in giving.

It took me a long time to learn the lesson of unconditional love. Every time my meditation teacher said the words 'love is giving, seeking nothing in return', I thought the guy was definitely out of his mind. For two years I just could not fathom the logic behind his statement. It made absolutely no sense to me. How could I give to someone who was abusive, how could I give to a friend who was not returning that friendship, how could I give my time and energy if I wasn't guaranteed a return? How?

Then universe sent me my son. I thought my child was going to be the most perfect angel born this side of heaven. I thought he was just going to lie there looking all peaceful and soft. I thought he would neatly fit into the scheme of my universe. The bigger universe had something else in mind for me. For the whole first year of his tiny existence my son cried, he screamed, he hollered. If it wasn't colic, it was his teething, if it was not his teething, he wanted attention. My son just loved to cry and I was a nervous wreck. I felt as though I was an actress in a B rate horror movie. I wanted universe to take my baby right on back to where he had come from. I wanted to stop giving. Of course, universe did not comply with my wishes. My son was staying. He was staying right where universe had chosen for him to be — with me on earth. So there it was I stuck with this crying baby. All sorts of horrible thoughts entered my mind. I wanted to give him up for adoption, pack him of to the Caribbean, or just simply chuck him out the window. I wanted to do everything but give to him. Wasn't giving about getting something back. All I was getting back was a bag of raw nerves. Not exactly my idea of fair returns.

Babies are helpless. As their mothers they rely on us for their first interpretation of the world, they rely on us for their nurturing, comfort and growing. They rely on us to turn them into men and women and so if I wasn't to crumble I had to learn to love. I had to give up all my old notions about love. I had to give to my son seeking nothing back in return. Like all first beginnings it was hard. Then the loving got easier. As it got easier I began to get the gifts universe had intended for me. I reached beyond my minds limits and reached into my well spring of unconditional love. Then the miracle happened — my small tormentor transformed into a beautiful, wise old spirit. His first beginnings became my abundant life lessons. Loving began to feel good.

Without unconditional love on the path the spiritual gems cannot be received. To love Unconditionally is not to love foolishly. it is not excuse to be beaten black and blue. It is not about having your needs dis-regarded or disrespected. Unconditional love on the journey is about walking the way with an open heart. It is about sending out light even when you think the person does not deserve it. Unconditional love is about letting go, forgiveness, seeing the lessons and moving on. It is giving without having the hidden agenda — to get. Bath under the fountain of unconditional and your life will always be watered. There will be no lack, no fear, no animosity, no loneliness. There will be no need to hold on for fear of losing the little you have. Trust and let unconditional love fill your empty spaces. Let it expand your heart. Let it heal your gaping wounds. Walk in with it and be blessed.

GOOD DEEDS AND WORDS

'What you send out is exactly what you get back.' 'What you send out is exactly what you get back.' Let these words become your mantra. Write them in big bold letters. Put them above your work station, your bathroom mirror, your bed head. Put them where you can see them. Internalise them in your daily living. Activate them in your life.

Always strive to have good words about someone. Always strive to do goodness towards the other person, the other woman, the other man. Never go out of your way to inflict your tongue or desire to act out your negative conditioning on someone else. Always bear in mind that meditation is about invoking harmony in all that you do and with all whom you interact. If you do not strive towards harmonious social relations you have defeated the purpose behind your practice, you have defeated the object to why you have been put here on earth.

As black women we can malicious, we can be hurtful, we can be mean when it comes to loving and supporting each other. All too often we find it easy to tear another sister down rather than bring her up. On the path it is important to remember that you are a child of God put here to act as a child of God. Your spirit has returned through your mother's womb not to create more chaos and friction in the world — there is enough of that. Not to create more distress — there is more human strife than mother earth can bear. You have returned with divine purpose, in divine time, to create divine peace.

It is time to stop the hurtful words. Examine what it is you are saying to your brothers and sisters. Examine the fear that feeds their fire. What is the fear motivating your gossip, wounding criticism and spiteful remarks? The time has come for you to put these destructive elements under the looking glass. It's time to understand them, embrace them and chuck them right out of your life. It is worthwhile to remember negative speech hurts someone else but above all it hurts you. It is hurts your quest for spiritual liberation. It hurts spirit's desire for growth.

Make a commitment to self, universe and spirit to create goodness wherever you are. There will be times when you will fall, when you will hurt someone with your deadly words or actions. Even when you fall, you can pick yourself up and try again.

Affirmation: 'my good words and deeds create goodness in my life'

POSITIVE THINKING

No one can suffer loss unless it be his own decisions.

No one suffers pain except his choice elects this for him.

No one can grieve nor fear nor think him sick unless these
are the outcomes he
And no one dies without his consent.
Nothing occurs but represents your wish,
and nothing is omitted that you choose.
A COURSE IN MIRACLES

Your thoughts and your thoughts only create your reality. Whatever you feel, think or imagine will be what you externally manifest and experience. Your world is your creation, not your mates, not your child's, not your friends, not the stranger's down the road. If you are lacking, it's because you believe you don't deserve. You have thought the thought, you have lived it out in your imagination and manifested its reality. If you are always attracting abusive relationships, deep down in your subconscious mind you are holding onto certain negative mental beliefs. You may believe there is something wrong with you, you do not contain innate goodness or there is nothing else out there but abusive men in the world.

When you hold a thought that limits your existence, that limits your universal expression, universe will send the thought right back to you just as you believe it to be. It will not be edited, re-shaped, re-written, adapted, condensed, amended or polished it will be received and returned just as spirit sent it out.

Positive thoughts will create for you positive

outcomes. Negative thoughts, on the other hand, will send you right into a ditch. Once in the hole of your own making you may want to blame everyone from your boyfriend, your mother, your father, your Auntie, your friend to your grandmother for your misfortune.

Accusations will inevitably start to fly: 'He did this to me', 'she did this to me', 'they did this to me'. I know because I've been there.

The next time you are plagued with negative thoughts repeat the affirmation: 'my beautiful thoughts create my beautiful reality.'

LETTING GO

'I release' are the simplest two powerful words you can utter on your journey. When you say 'I release' with all your heart you are sending out a statement to universe indicating your readiness for change. When said 'I release' will usher forth your dynamic spiritual un-foldment.

At first ' I release' will feel hard to say: your teeth will clench, stomach churn, head hurt. Ego will fight back. The answer is to release and surrender. Surrender wears the hard edge of resistance down. When resistance is worn down ego has to get out.

'Whatever you are trying to release on your path, say 'I release' and surrender. Surrender to the eternal power. Surrender and ease God in. Fill your heart with love. Breath. Trust and release.

INHALE. EXHALE

I release and know I am an energetic force for change.
I release and accept I am supported by the universe
I release and I am purified.
I release, I release, I release.
I release the old and make room for the new
I release all limitations as I embrace expansion
I release anger. I embrace love
I release jealously. I embrace acceptance
I release the old negative emotions that conspire to destroy me as I embrace the new ones that build.
I release. I release. I release.

INHALE. EXHALE

SELFLESSNESS

Divine law states: each and everyone of God's children is from the same seed. Each divine manifestation of God belongs to the same universal fabric of life. As children of God we are bonded together by the universal threads of ones.

Whatever you do, whatever you say, whichever way you choose to act will affect not only you — it will affect your mother, brother, husband, son, daughter, friend, stranger, lover. Your actions, words and deeds will reverberate to everything around and beyond your personal universe. Understanding this will help you to grasp the universal law of selflessness. Selflessness on the path is the full cup of compassion and kindness for your fellow man, your fellow woman. It is the dictum which will expand you beyond the restricts of the personal 'I' into the universal 'us'.

Selflessness does not imply as popular myth would have us believe: your needs, desires, emotions and wants must be ignored. It does not empower those around you to take you for granted. To be selfless is to exchange yourself with others in the understanding that we are all one and we are all unique. To live out its essence is to partake in a divine way of being, a divine way of thinking, a divine way of acting, a divine way of doing things which goes beyond 'stupid folly' and 'blind giving.'

Put on your selfless shoes — walk a good path, an abundant path, a path of enlightenment. Walk with the understanding — you are one with all things. Walk in the abundant flow of universe. Walk with peace. Walk and know in the universal scheme of ones life ain't out to get you. You are not alone in your suffering, in your growing, in your life lessons. Together we share in the same scheme of things through the universal breath.

Whenever you are tempted to fall to ego's self focused mantras: 'why me', 'she/he does not like me', 'I feel so alone in my pain, my hurt, my suffering' — inhale. Exhale and know that you are supported in the ones of universe.

Repeat the affirmation:

I am part of the divine scheme of universal ones. I am a divine child of God and treat others, as such. I am part of the divine scheme of universal ones.

I am a divine child of God and know that I am supported. I am part of the divine scheme of universal ones.

I am a divine child of God and know that I am not alone.

In all that I do I give selflessly, I give of myself, I give with compassion, I give with love, I give with understanding, I give with joy, I give asking seeking nothing in return.

I give and in my giving I accept whatever I give I give back to myself. If I give love, I receive love. If I give hate I receive hate. If I give understanding so will I receive.

I commit to magnificence

I commit to all of the above and more knowing that my selfless attitude is the provider of all of my needs.

ASKING

It takes me forever to say my prayers these days, but I don't care, because this time around, I want to make sure God doesn't have to do any guesswork.

TERRY MCMILLAN

One week of my life, I sat in darkness, hunger and misery. Simply put, I had no money, no food in my cupboard, no electricity on my meter. I was depressed, frustrated, feeling very poor and too proud to ask for help.

Why as black women do we find it so hard to ask for what we need. Why do we feel so ashamed, so vulnerable to admit we cannot do it all, all of the time. There are times when we just need to ask for some help. When we need to put our Pride away in its little box and announce to the world: I am vulnerable, I am needy, I am in need.

The ability to ask for help is a prerequisite for walking the path. As you dust, clean, and tidy house you will confront fear, pain, hurt, anger, anticipation, anxiety, denial, tears — you will have many moments when you will need the strength to carry on with your inner journey of transformation. This strength may have to come from a friend, partner or family member. It may have to be called down from universe. Wherever the source, it can only be received when you breath and ask.

Try it now. In the quiet and solitude of your own time and space practice asking for help. Repeat these words inwardly and several times: 'I need help'. Now manifest their existence externally to the world. Say them softly and make them grow larger and louder in the energy of conviction.

When you ask for the help you need you will open your universe up to a multitude of divine possibilities. Through surrender you will receive the blessings you have blocked with resistance — with the 'I am a strong black woman' attitude.

Next time you find yourself in desperation, in need of reassurance, a little warmth, a little comfort, a little sweetness on the way why don't you get down on your knees and pray — acknowledge the presence of your indwelling divine intelligence and its omnipotent ability to help you on your way.

When you pray get down on your right knee, put your right hand over your heart, your left hand in the air, with the left thumb under the base of the left little finger. This is the ancient Egyptian prayer position of respect and submittance to God Father, God Mother.

Close your eyes. Inhale. Exhale. Focus. What is it you need to ask for? Is it wisdom? Is it guidance? Is it support? Whatever it is, know that every word you speak is an energy sound being imprinted into the energy bed of universal consciousness. Know that when what you ask for is in tune with the divine order of things: has no intent of hurt, no intent of manipulation, no intent of causing grief, no intent of gain for gain sake — your prayers will be listened to and answered.

GRATITUDE

> *We live by the good fortune of what heaven and earth provide. We make our offering to show our gratitude.*
>
> DENG MING-DAO

Who have you said thank you to recently? What have you given back as a sign of your gratitude?

Gratitude on the path is a must. It is a necessary requirement to continued receiving. It is a magnanimous sign of humility. A giving gift of acknowledgement. Gratitude can be given back with two simple words — Thank You.

Libation and ancestral offerings are ways we traditionally showed our gratitude for the higher support we receive in our lives.

LIBATION

To pour libation you will need:
A wooden bowl or glass.
Spring water.
A plant.
A prayer of thank you.
Names of family ancestors you feel have been guiding you in your journey.
Names of nation ancestors: Malcolm X, Harriet Tubman, Rosa Parker etc. who have helped to uplift you.

THE SEQUENCE OF YOUR LIBATION

Beginning:
You can stand or kneel on your right knee with your right hand over your heart.
Inhale. Exhale for a few minutes.
Close your eyes and focus.

Thank out aloud:
The most high for the guidance, blessings and wisdom you have received.
Your family ancestors for their help: put this in your own special words.
The nation ancestors for their help: put this in your own special words.

End
Pour your water into the earth of the plant or on the ground.

Make libation a daily ritual. Pour it every morning before you do anything else. Make universal acknowledgement your first act for the day.

GIFT GIVING
Every day I put melon on my female healing shrine, every week I buy flowers in offering for my guiding ancestors and the most high. Gift giving is a beautiful way to show our appreciation for the miracles we receive everyday. Your gift can be small, or big. It can be something you buy from the shop or something you make. Whatever your gift is, it is important you give it with a sincere heart.

9: AFFIRMATION

> *I used to think that I could not go*
> *And life was nothing but an awful song*
> *But now I know the meaning of true love*
> *I am leaning on the everlasting arms*
> *If I can see it, then I can do it*
> *If I just believe it there is nothing to it.*
>
> *I believe I can fly, I believe I can touch the sky*
> *I think about it every night and day*
> *Spread my wings and fly away, I believe I can soar*
> *I see me running through the open door*
> *I believe I can fly, I believe I can fly*
> *I believe I can fly.*
>
> R. KELLY
> *I Believe I Can Fly*

INHALE. EXHALE.

You are at total peace. You are filled with the fragrance of renewed vital energy. You have let go of the old and embraced the new. You have taken responsibility and committed self to growth. You have decided to get out of a limited groove and touch base with POWER.

INHALE. EXHALE.

Now it is time to affirm the journey you have made. It is time to commit, reflect, and integrate all the life lessons you have learnt on the way. It is time to celebrate the journey you will continue to make. It is time to give thanks.

INHALE. EXHALE.

MIRROR, MIRROR

Let's go back to the mirror exercise you did in chapter 1. The purpose now is to review how far you have come since that first encounter. If you feel it is not very far, that's okay. There is no spiritual competition on the road to dynamic emergence. Acknowledge where you are at. Embrace your growth. Make a firm commitment to your continued ascension into a new higher self.

EXERCISE
You will need:
    A mirror.
    Five minutes down time.
    Quiet space.

Take a few moments to centre your self in your breath. Allow your breath to become slow and rhythmic. When you are ready hold the mirror up to your face and look deeply into it. What do you see, how do you feel about the person you are now looking at? If you are having difficulties looking, that's okay. Don't hurry yourself. Acknowledge where you are at. Inhale your discoveries. Embrace them with spirit. Record them in your spiritual journal.

As you continue to look into the mirror, affirm to self: 'I am perfect just as I am'. Perfection does not mean there is no room for a commitment to continued growth.

INHALE. EXHALE.

LOVE LETTER

When was the last time you wrote a love letter to self. Uhmm, that long ago. A love letter is something we most often write to loved ones. In it we affirm how wonderful they are, the things they have done for us that make us feel good, the journey they have taken us on. We affirm our love for them and our gratitude.

Affirm your journey now. Write a love letter to self. In it acknowledge your sacred transformations. Give thanks to universe for its tireless support. Send loving light to spirit.

Before writing, spend quiet time with self. Use this time to reflect on the process you have been through. To help you, review the spiritual journal you have been keeping. Use its notes to help guide you in what to write. Below is a prototype of how your letter should look:

> *Dear self,*
> *Thank you for:*

Para 1: *The Recognition of* — followed by your thoughts

Para 2: *The Release from* — followed by your thoughts

Para 3: *The Connection to* — followed by your words

Para 4: *I commit to*: followed by your words

Thank you

Signature

Address the letter to your home address. Repeat this exercise every three months.

How did it feel to write a love letter to self? Did it feel strange? Did it feel stupid? Did it feel just down right ridiculous? Did you have mixed feelings about doing it? Did you feel in tune with writing beautiful acknowledgments to yourself straight away?

Whatever you felt about writing your love letter will further indicate where you are at in your travels. If you found it a struggle, a challenge or near impossible to write, that's okay. Its an exercise you will repeat more than once on your journey.

INHALE. EXHALE

GRATITUDE PRAYER

Affirmation is also a time for giving thanks for universal support received. Spend a few moments in quiet time as you say a prayer of gratitude to the divine intelligence. Let your gratitude come from your heart. Here is some guidance on what your prayer can sound like.

Dear Father, Mother
I submit to your divine intelligence. I acknowledge you as the essence of all life.
Thank you for all you have done for me.
Thank you for all you have shared with me.
Thank you for your guidance.

Thank you for your wisdom.
Thank you for your clarity.
Thank you for helping me to walk along my path with strength and uprightness.
Thank you for helping to see the things that have been blocking me from you my higher self.
Thank you for helping me to embrace my limitations.
Thank you for giving me the courage to begin the process of change.
Thank you.
Thank you.
Thank you.
Amen.

INHALE. EXHALE.

SACRED ARROW
I learnt about the native American Indians arrow making tradition when on a retreat in London. I found it to be of such power I would like to include it here.

You will need:

Quiet space.

A slim piece of wood — preferably one gathered from mother nature. The wood must be dry.

A carving knife.

Wood glue.

Decorative objects: shells, ribbons, gems, crepe paper, an assortment of different types of material, paint etc.

The process:

The making of the arrow ritual does not literally mean you make a conventional arrow. It is a ritual designed to connect you to your essential nature. It is a meditation that takes you on an internal journey. In quiet space you will to let spirit guide you on what to do with the piece of wood you have collected or bought. You may find you have an urge to shape, carve, and decorate it. You may so like its natural state you keep your alterations down to the minimum.

Whatever you find yourself doing with the wood you are transforming you will learn about the way you travel. You will learn about the things that keep you back: fear, lack of trust, the need to be in control etc. You will discover the principle you need to forward you on your path towards a higher state of being. That principle may be courage, faith, love, trust, nurturing, kindness, hope etc. whatever principle comes to you will be unique to your life journey.

Give yourself plenty of time to complete the process. Keep your journal to hand. Write down the thoughts and feelings you have while on your journey. When you have finished re-read your notes. Reflect. What did you discover about the way you travel? What principle did you discover you need to take you into the next phase of your growth? That is the principle your arrow will represent. You may have found that you harbour a lot of fear about your future and you need courage to take your next step forward. In this case your arrow will represent courage.

Once completed your sacred arrow must be treated as such. It must be stored in a special bag or piece of cloth and safely stored away. It is to taken out only when you feel you are in need of the strength of the principle is represents for you. Hold it. Focus. Breath and embrace the strength it holds for you.

MY SACRED ARROW DIARY EXTRACT

My process of making the arrow feels like love in action. It feels like a journey to a place of peace.

Working on the arrow with other women is a good process. Although we are working on the arrow together we are each in our own sacred space doing our own thing. I'm not looking at the other woman and she is not looking at me. We're not in competition. We're just in our own moment carving something from nature and working with its beauty while enjoying the transformation.

Working on the arrow is a journey of patience, concentration and focus. It is a restful journey with meaning. It is a journey of clearing the mind of distracting thoughts. It's a journey of trust. You don't

know what you are making or how it will come out.
But you trust and you make the journey. The end
result is always beautiful. Always complete. It is also
A journey of creativity. A journey that takes me into
another way of doing things.

I know the arrow is complete. It is a journey of
knowing when ends have arrived. I feel tired. It is
tiring journeying but I feel at peace, I feel rested, I feel
as if I have learnt through the power of sacred
connection.

BLESSIN' WE

As part of a bride's preparation for marriage in parts
of West Africa, her feet must be bathed in scented
water laced with sacred herbs. In acknowledgement
of the journey she must make from singledom to
married life her feet are washed as female friends and
relatives nurture her with words of encouragement,
sound marital advice and loving affirmations.

On the spiritual path our feet are symbolic of the
road we must travel. Sometimes the road will be
covered in stones, sometimes it will protected by
feathers. However the road appears you must have
the courage and conviction to walk it. You must have
the devotion to see your journey through. The clarity
of vision to step through the fear, the hurt, the pain,
the anxiety, the anticipation, the confusion, the
distractions — which will want to throw you off
course. Know that your feet — symbolic of spirit —
will take you where you need to go.

The foot blessing ritual is our final affirmation.

Repeat it any time you need the courage to move on.

You will need:

A quiet space

15-30 minutes down time.

A bowl of warm water scented with your favourite aromatic oil.

Place your feet in the bowl

INHALE. EXHALE. Allow your breath to take you into a deep state of relaxation

When you are ready, visualise yourself walking your path with courage and confidence. As you do so see yourself growing more powerful, more centred, more sure in the knowledge of divine truth. At the end of your visualisation allow yourself to become engulfed by a white light. Its descent begins from the crown of your head down to the tip of your toes. Feel its cool protective touch surround and empower spirit. As you near the end of your meditation begin to lovingly wash your feet while you Repeat this affirmation several times or an affirmation of your choice: I am guided by the loving light of the Divine Grace. In this knowledge I walk my path with peace, harmony, and vision.

INHALE. EXHALE.

> *I had no idea what I was going to make of my life, but I had given a promise and found my innocence. I swore I'd never lose it again.*
> **MAYA ANGELOU,** *Gather Together in My Name*

Space for your thoughts

....
....
....
....
....
....
....
....
....
....
....
....
....
....
....
....
....
....
....
....
....
....
....
....
....

Space for your thoughts

Space for your *thoughts*

....
....
....
....
....
....
....
....
....
....
....
....
....
....
....
....
....
....
....
....
....
....
....
....
....
....

....
....
....
....
....
....
....
....
....
....
....
....
....
....
....
....
....
....
....
....
....
....
....
....
....
....
....

Space for your thoughts

....
....
....
....
....
....
....
....
....
....
....
....
....
....
....
....
....
....
....
....
....
....
....
....
....
....

Space for your thoughts

ACTS OF INSPIRATION
By Justina Wokoma

It's all too easy to lose sight of what we really want out of life, and to keep the motivation to attain these goals, *Acts of Inspiration* is a collection of daily meditations which helps us stay on track. Packed with thought provoking quotations and spiritual insights, this book really is a life changing experience.

Author **Justina Wokoma** explores the power of the human spirit and shows us how to positively harness the life energy that flows through every one of us. *Acts of Inspiration* is an essential guide for those on the journey to reclaim their sense of self-purpose and direction.

Nigerian born, **Justina Wokoma** (28) quit her physics degree course to explore the spiritual aspects of herself and her heritage - *Acts of Inspiration* is the result. London based Justina, has spent many years studying traditional West African culture and spirituality which has greatly influenced her writing.

The wisdom and insight of many black inspirational leaders, philosophers, artists and other achievers are chronicled toghether for the first time in this unique book. For the growing number of people who realise that material success is meaningless without spiritual growth, this book is essential reading.

Published by The X Press.
£7.99